Snazzy

Angie's Patterns - Volume 3

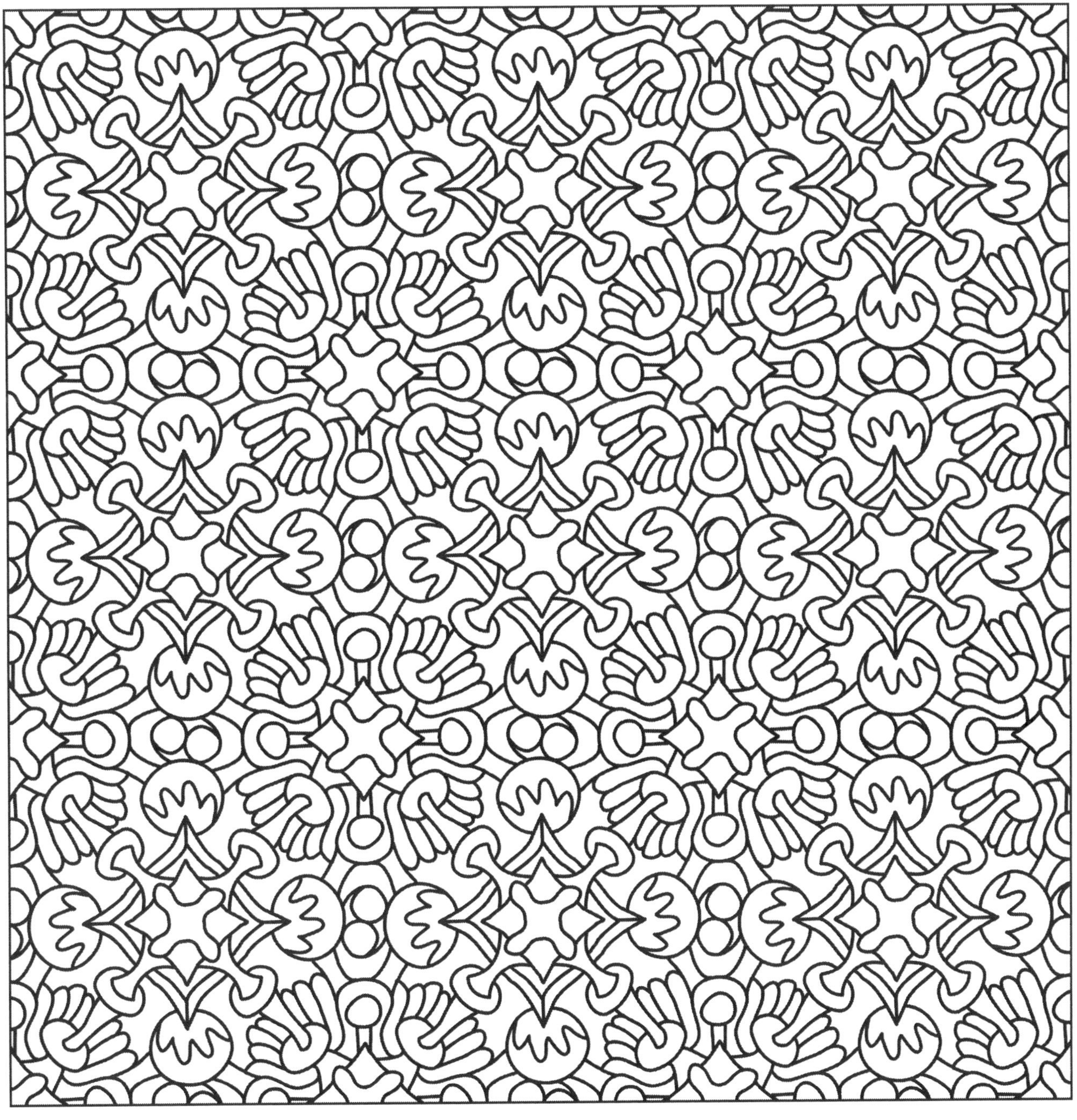

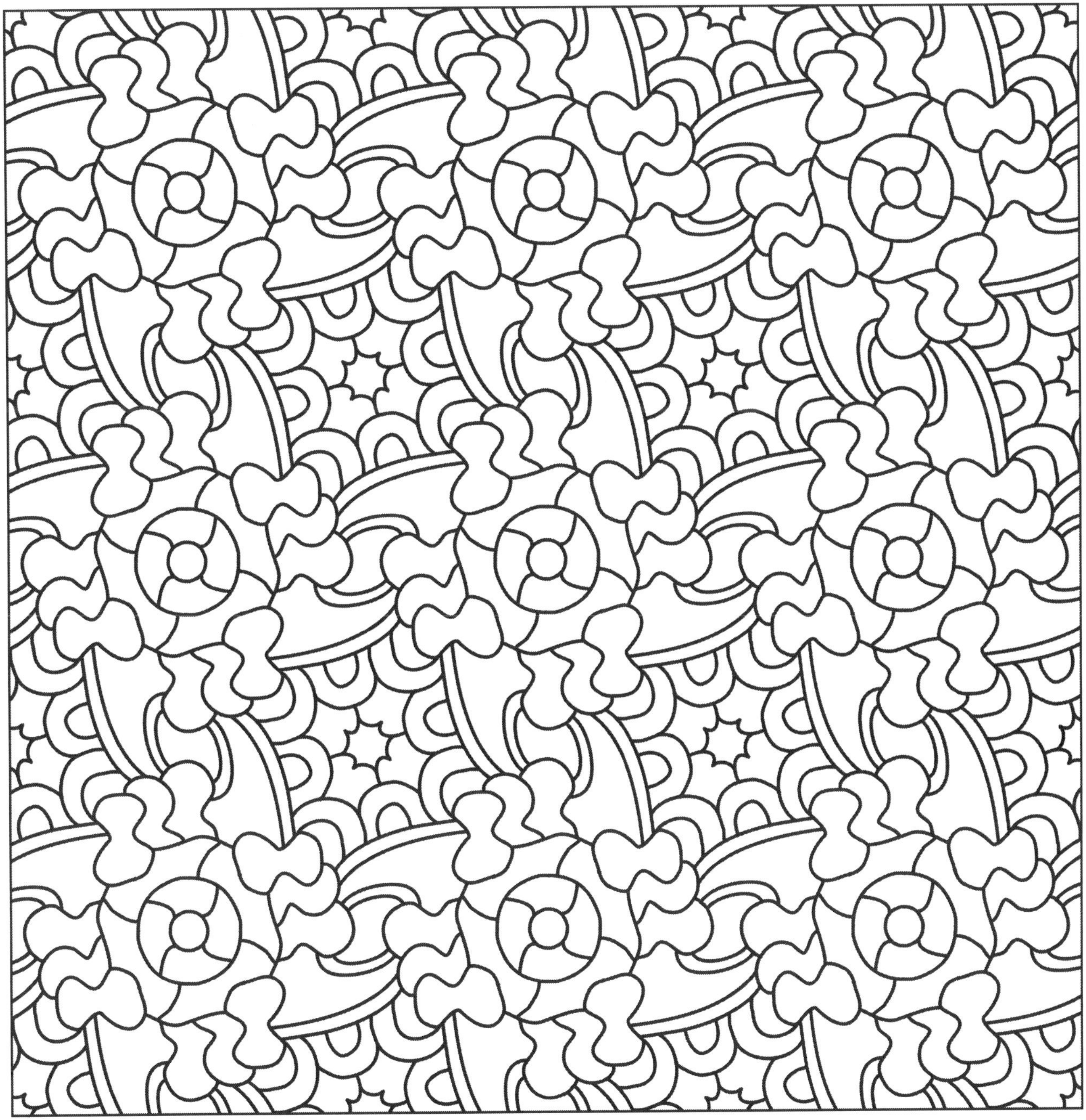

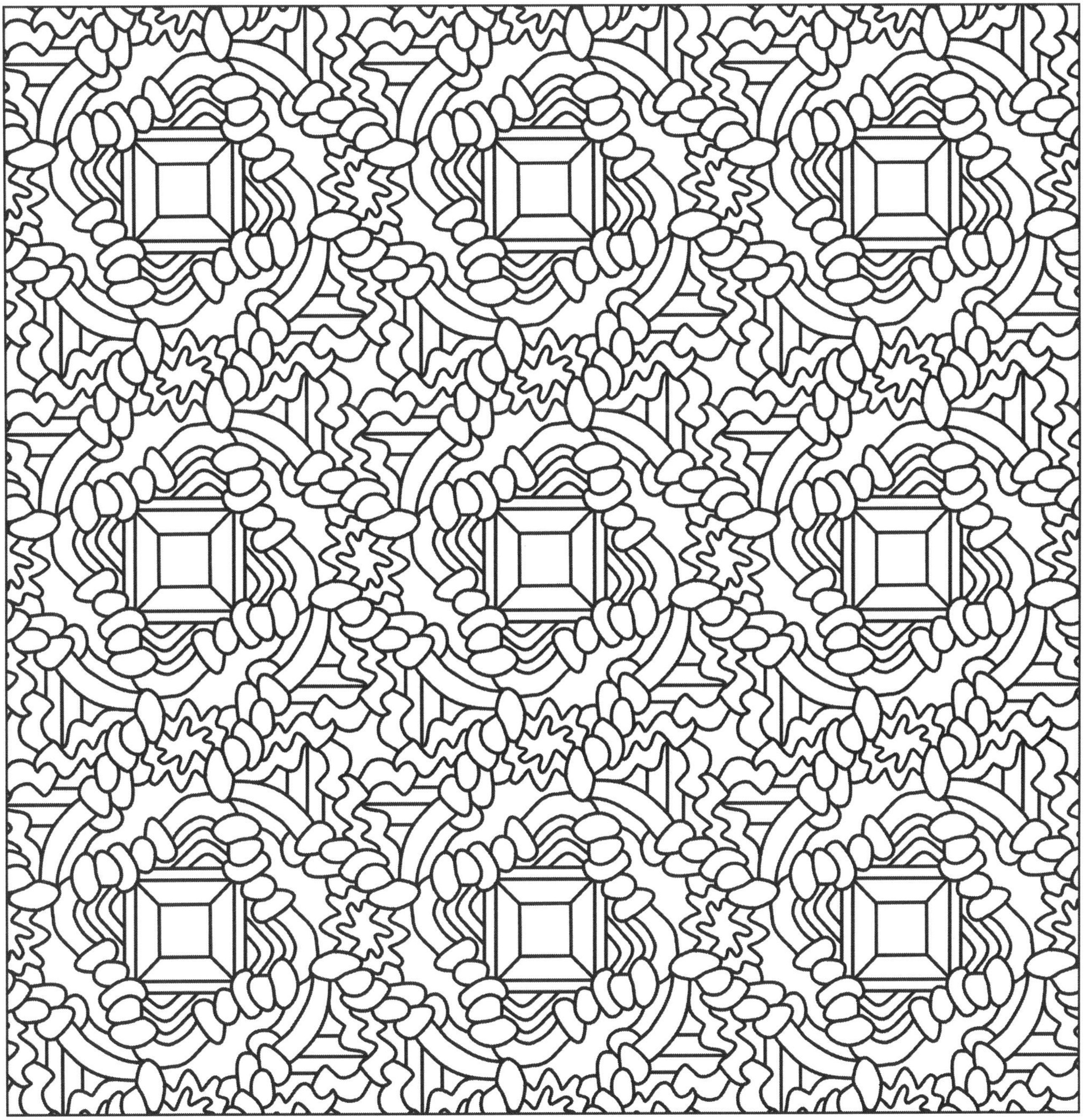

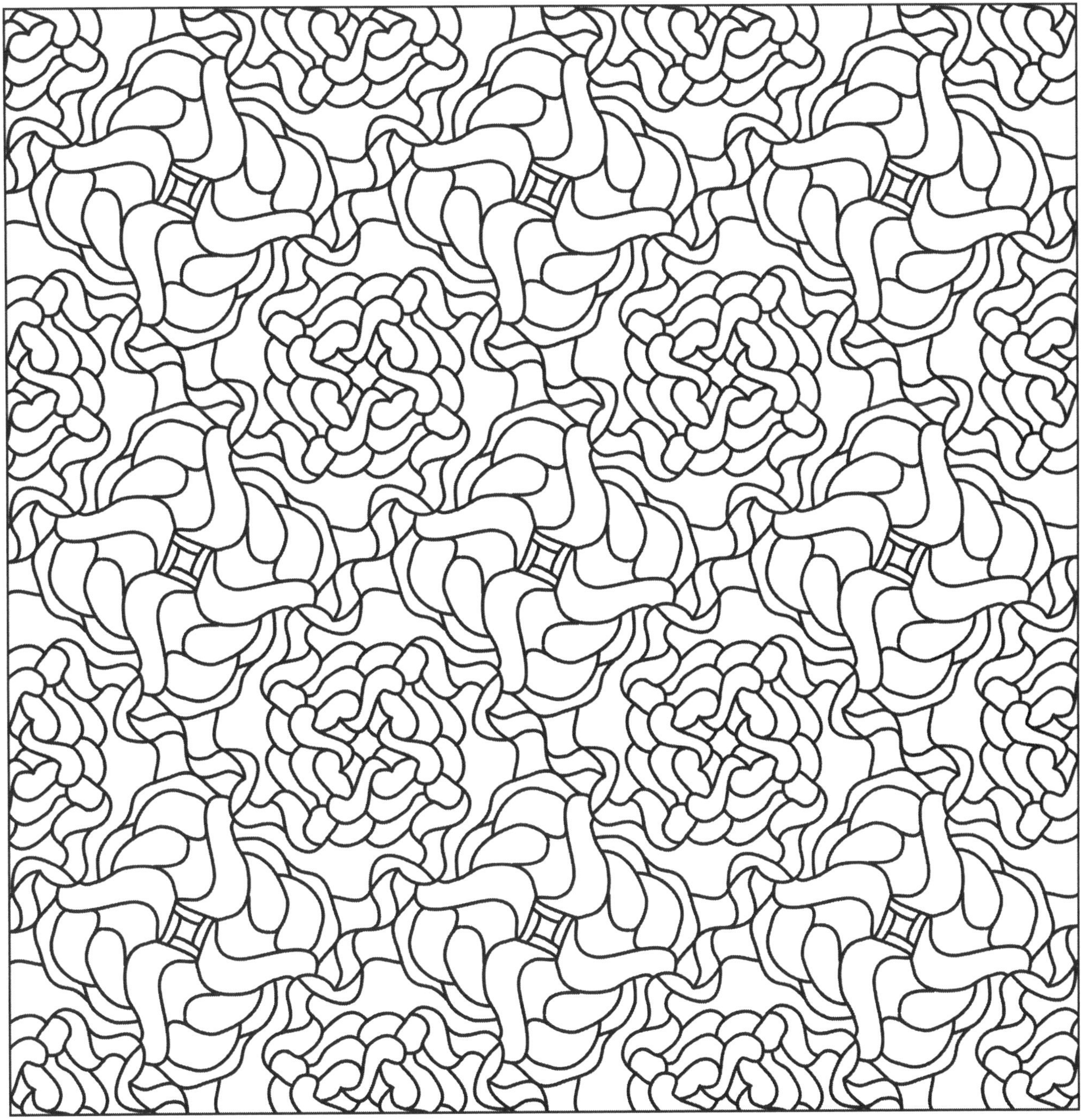

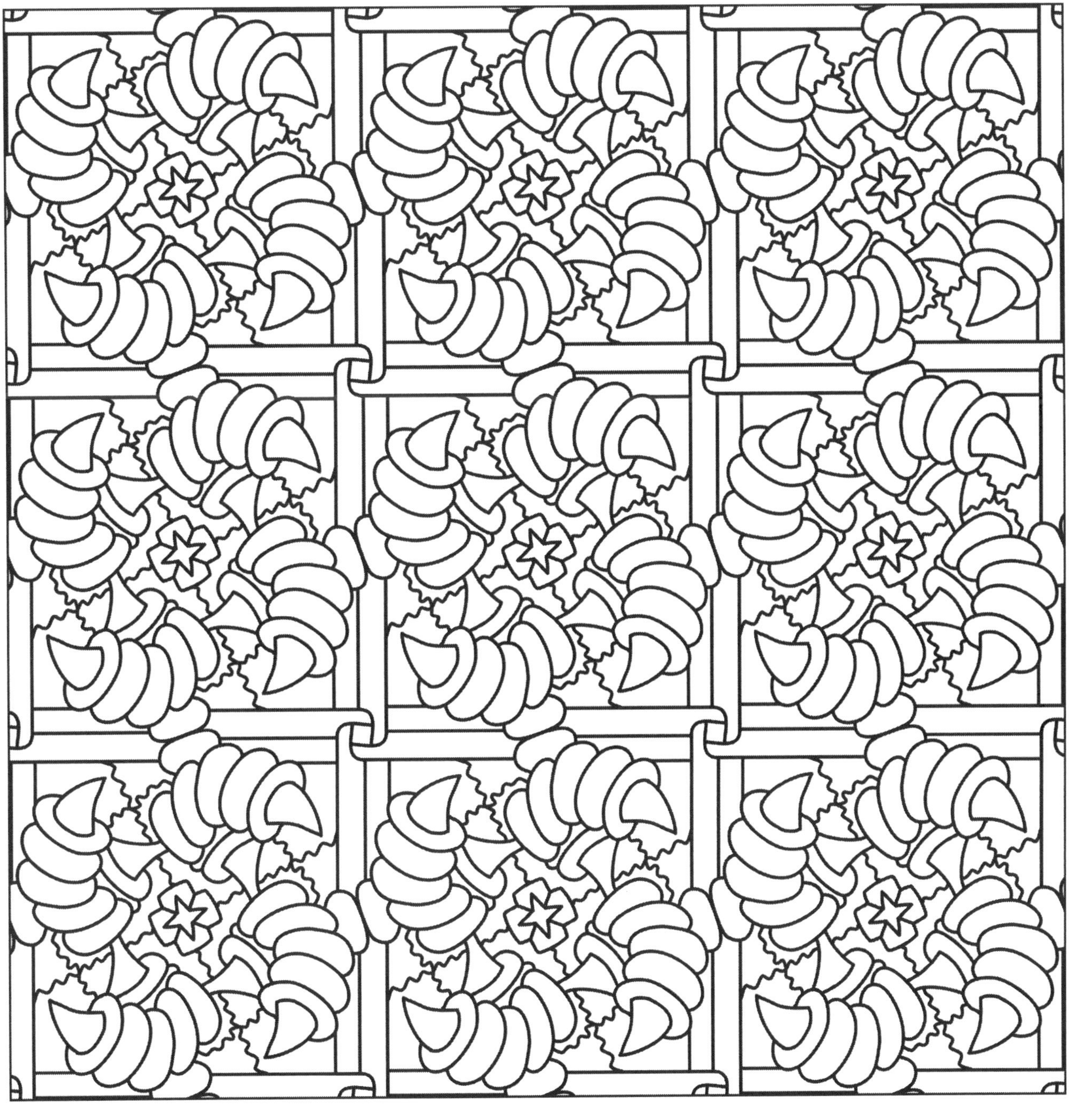

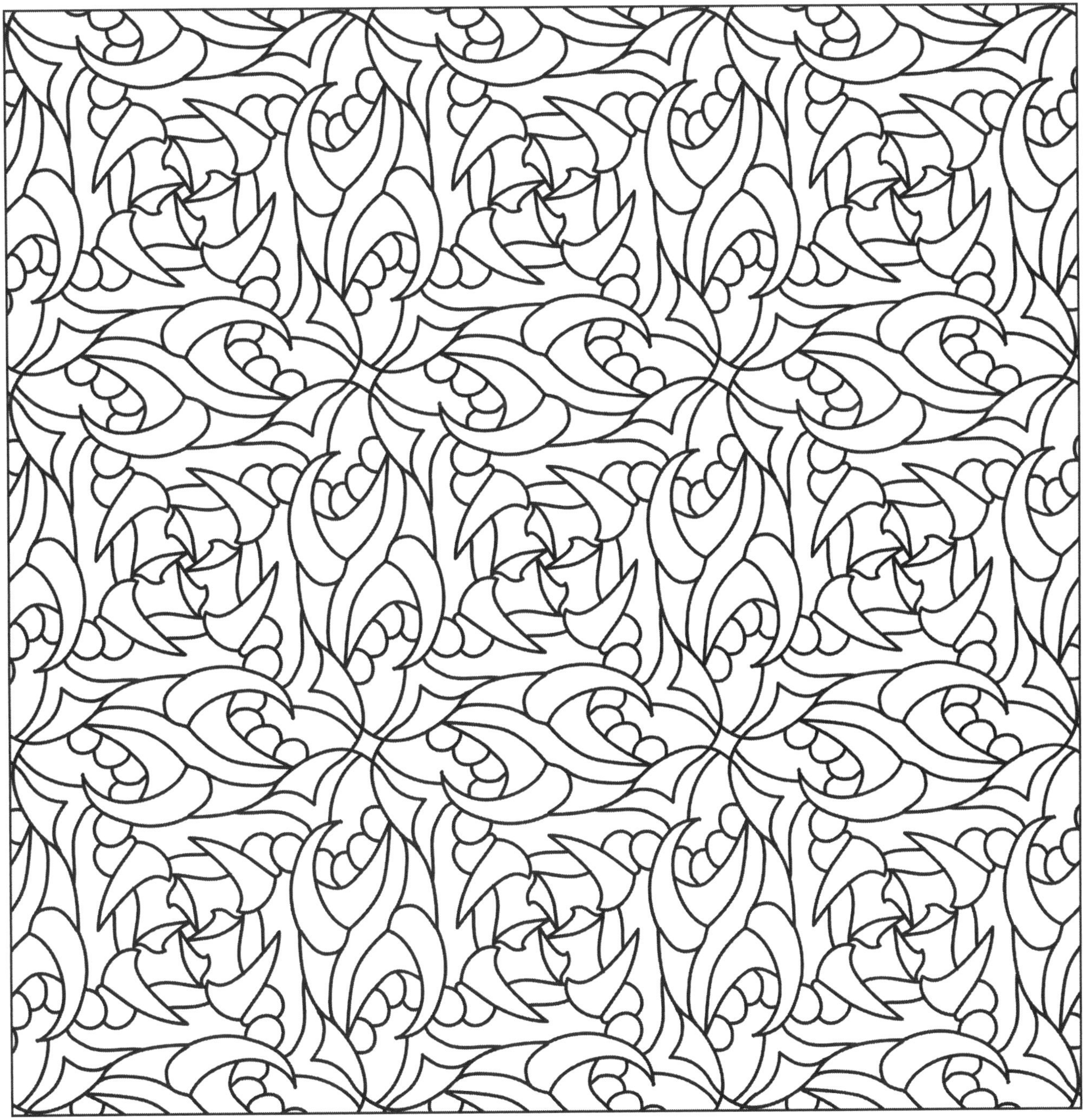

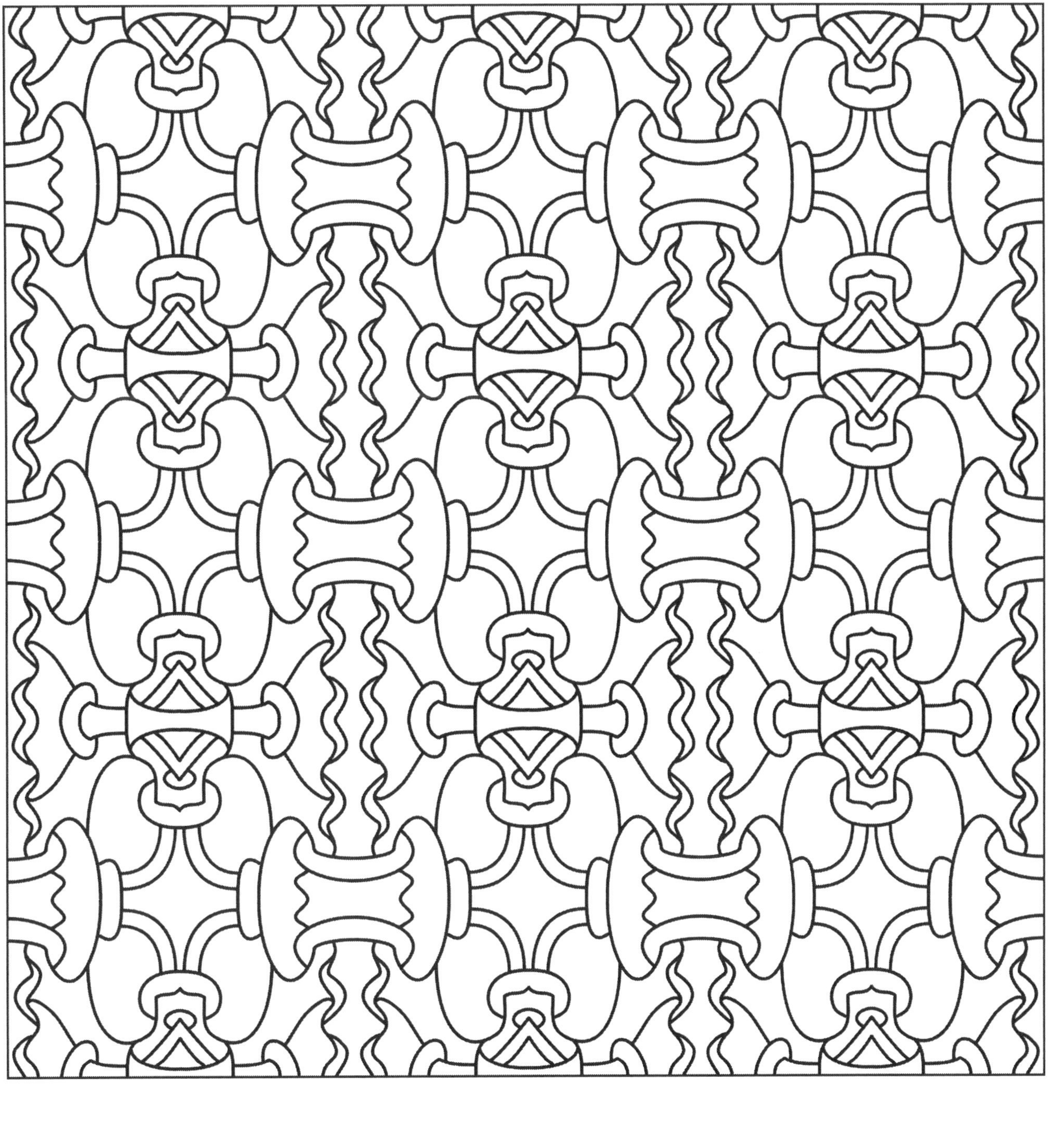

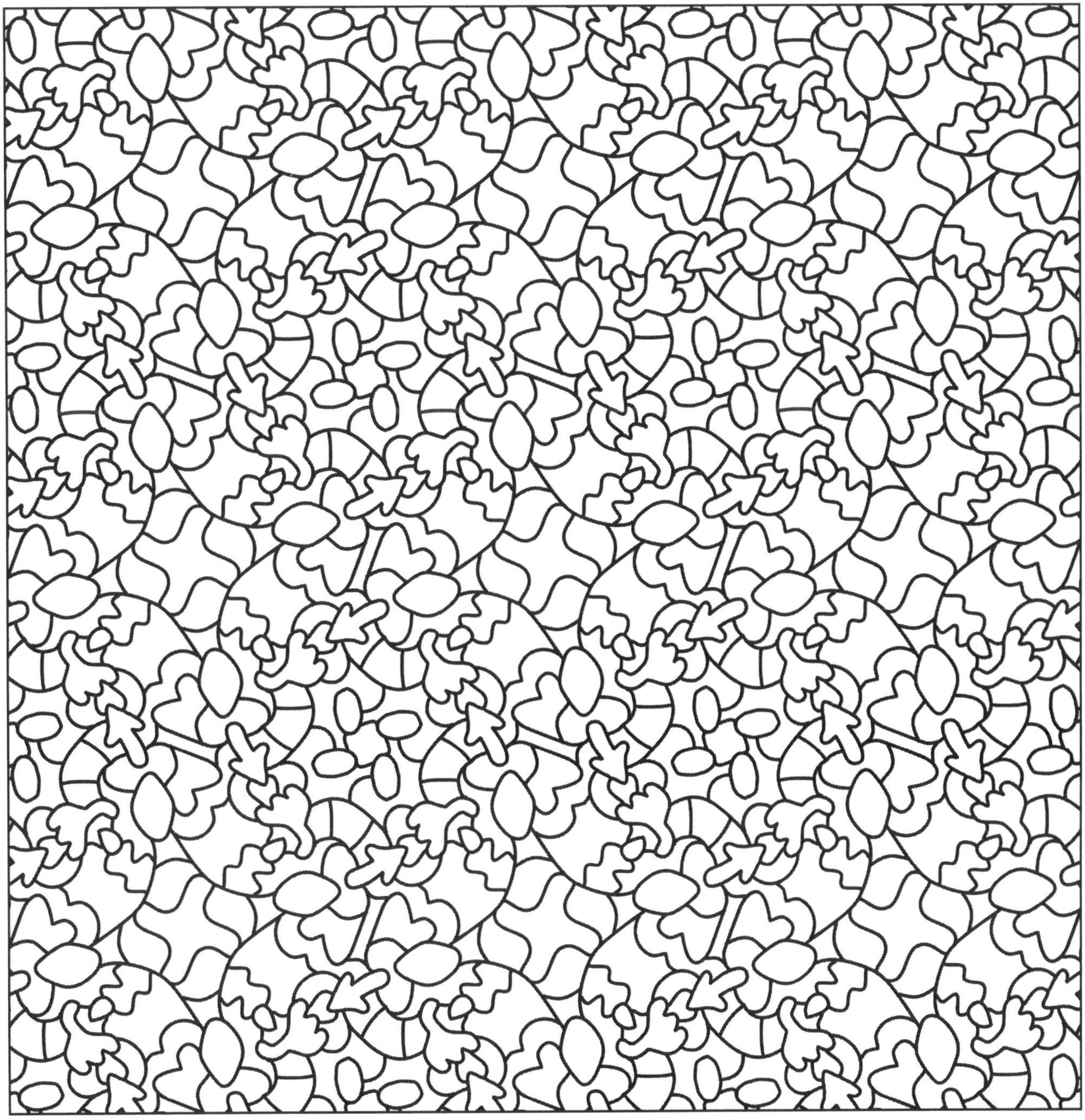

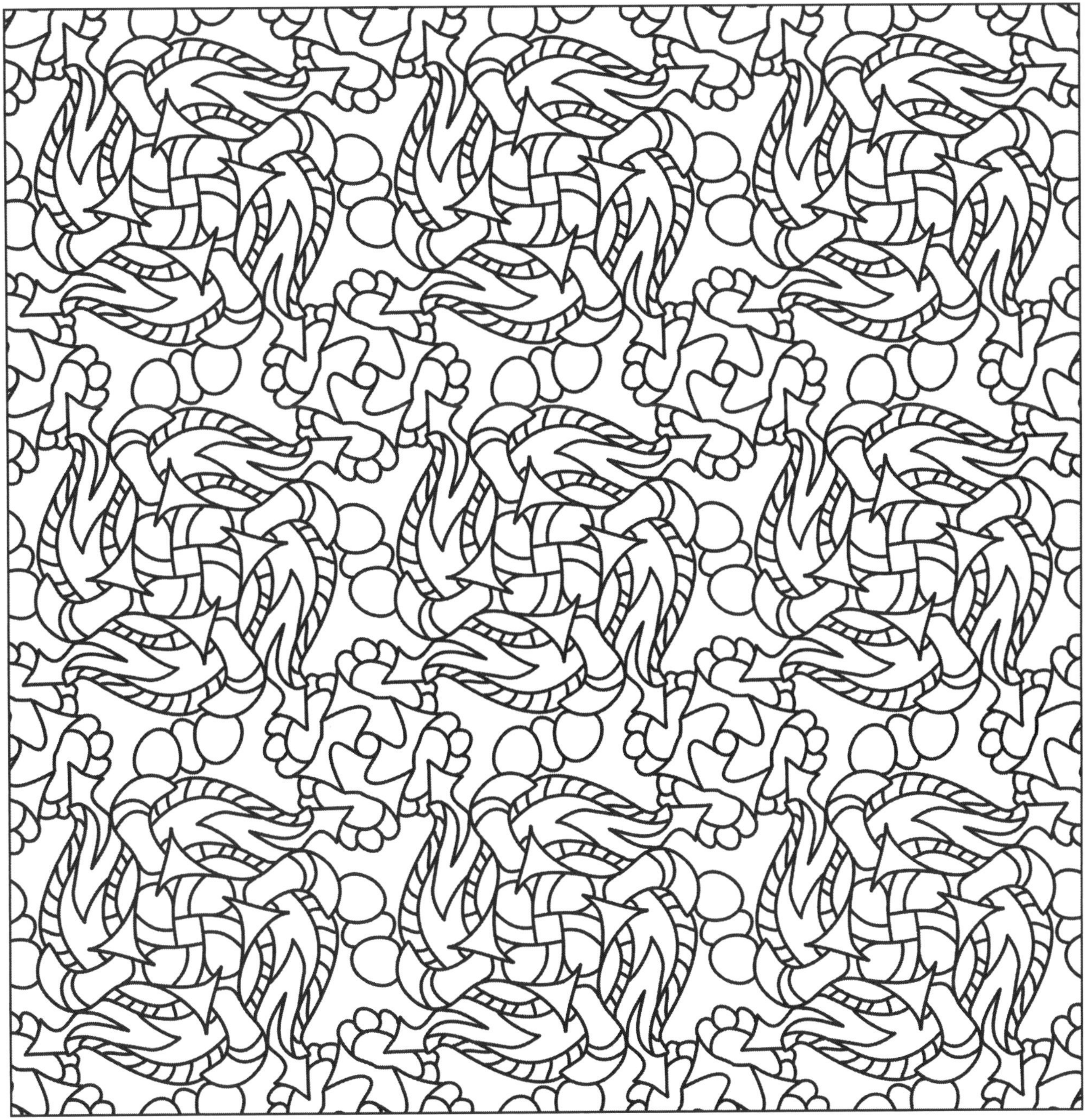

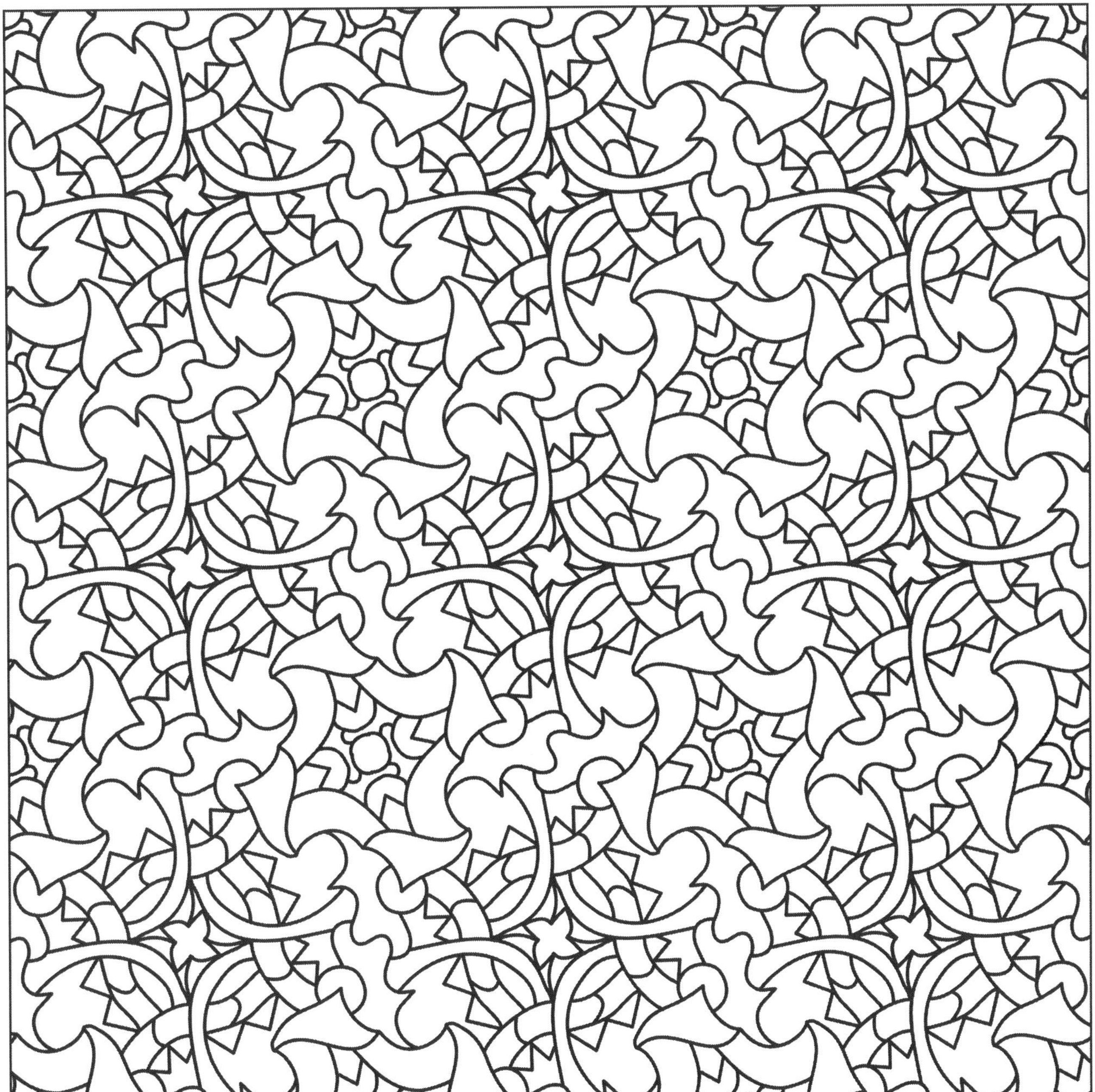

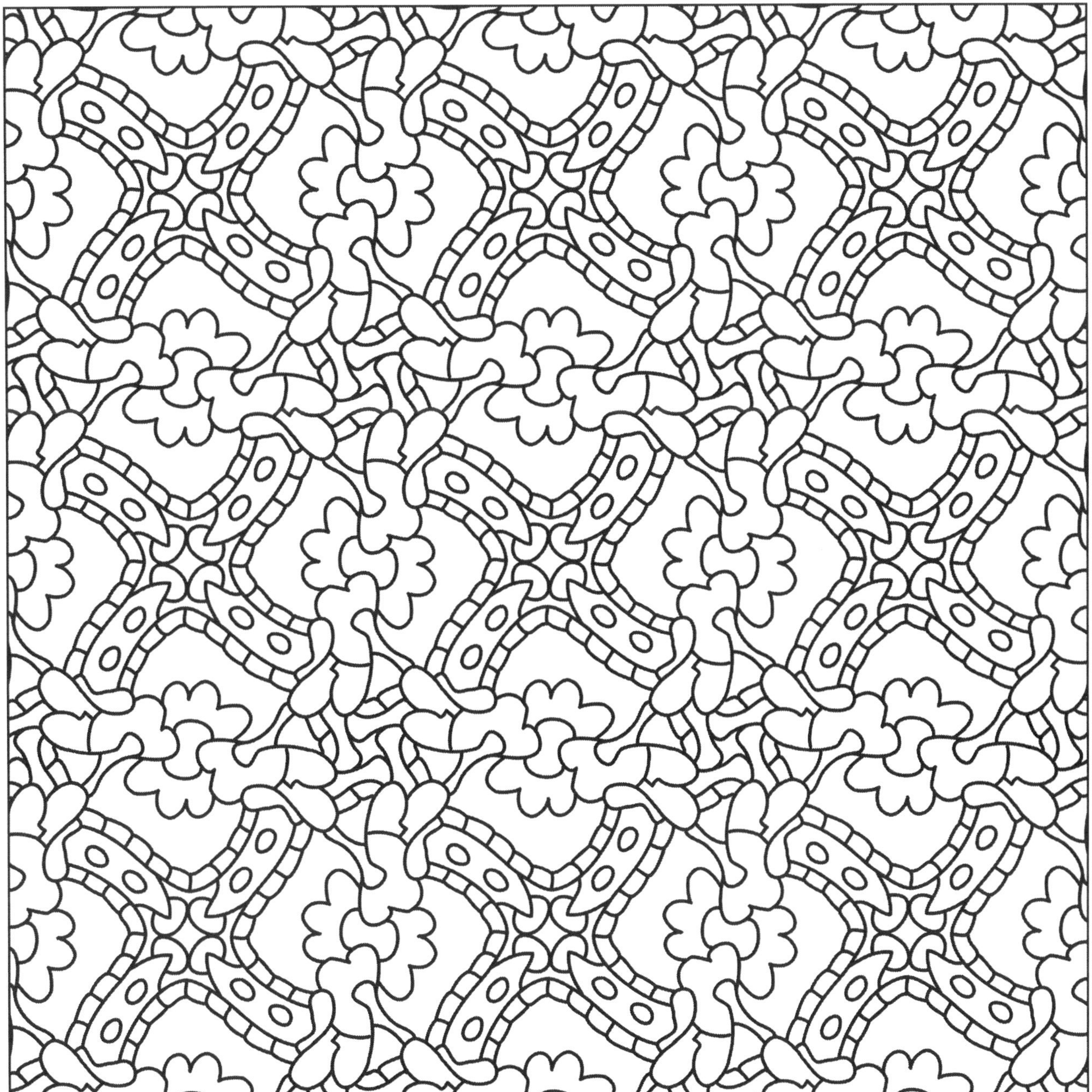

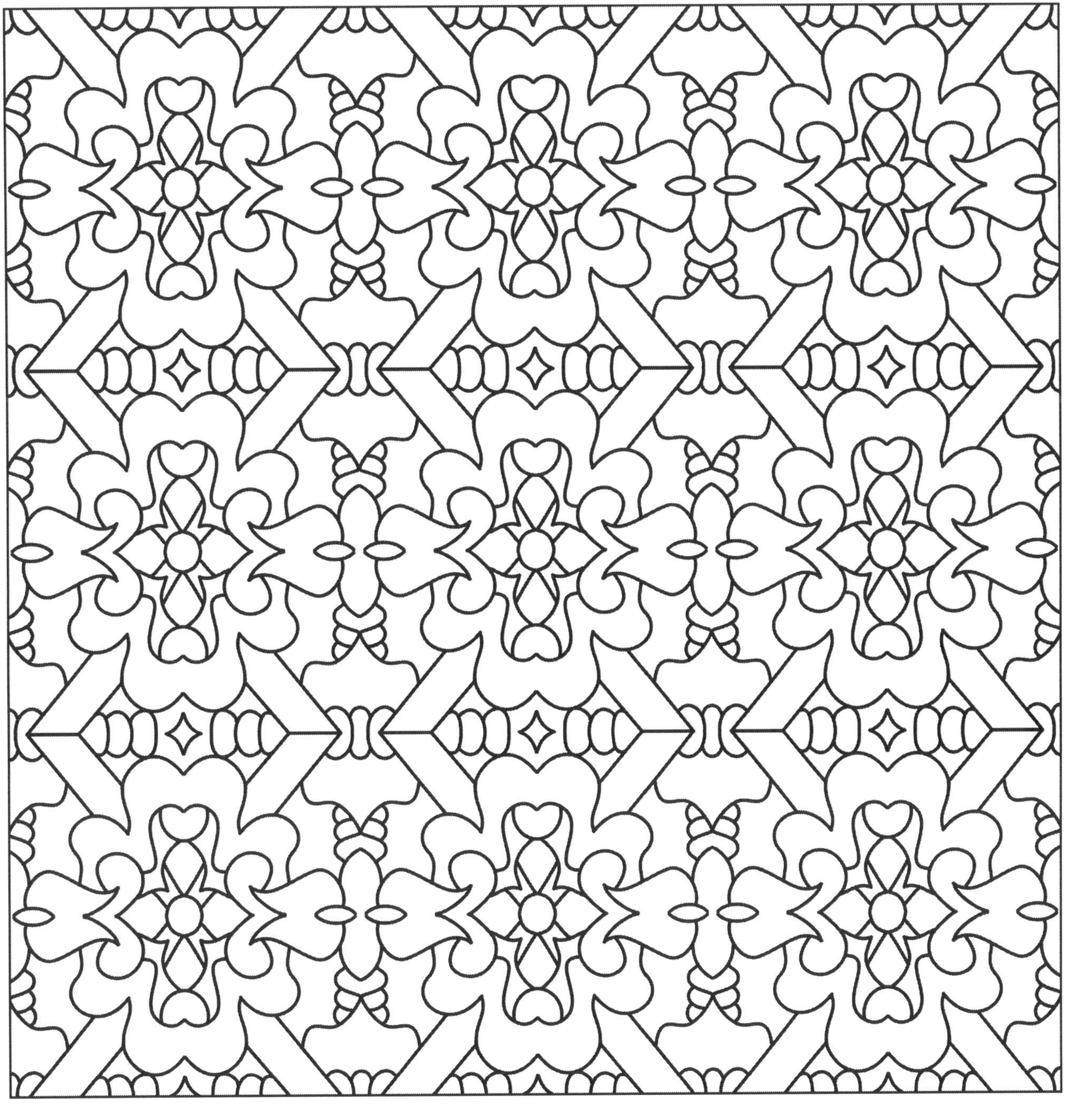

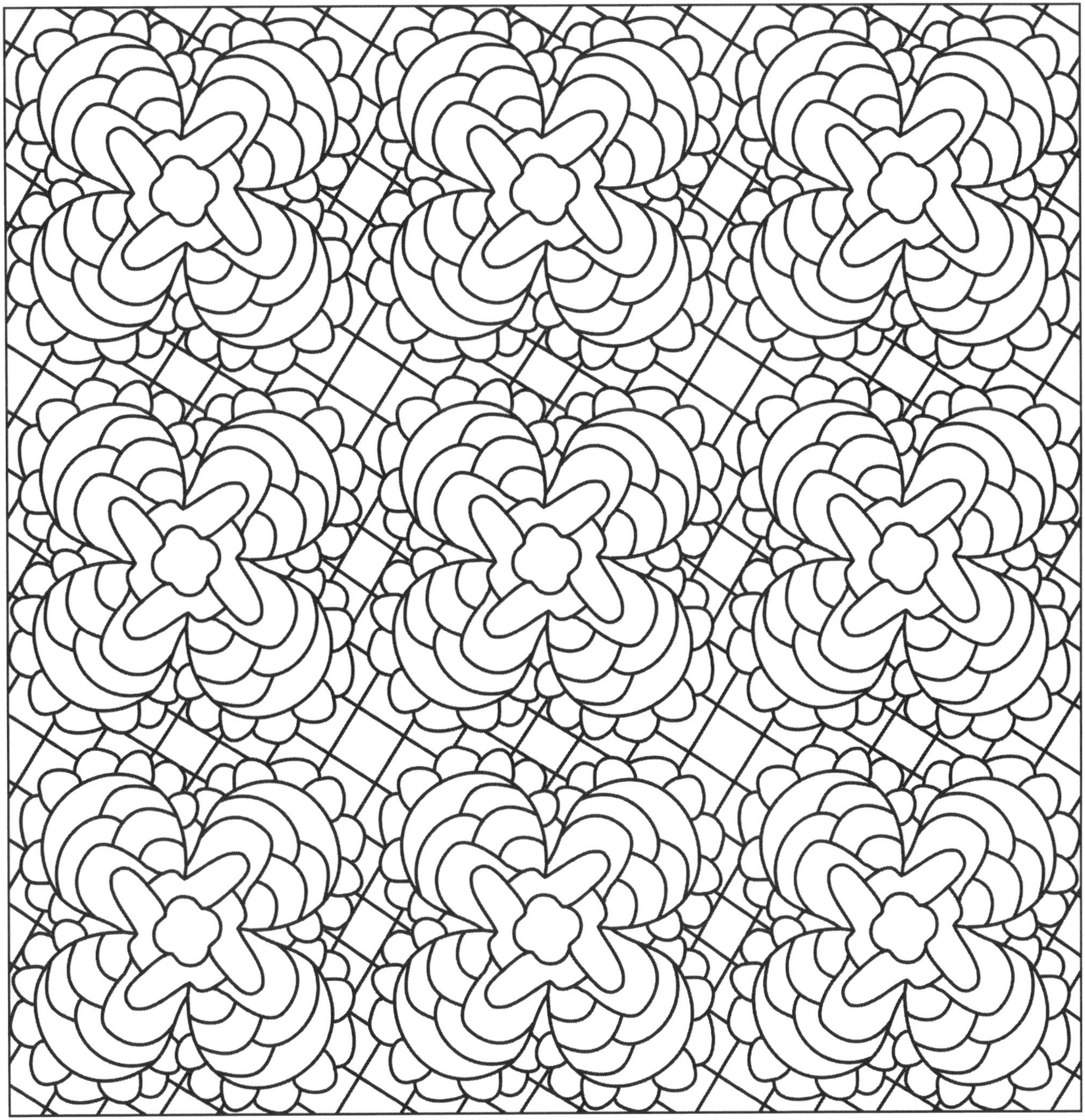

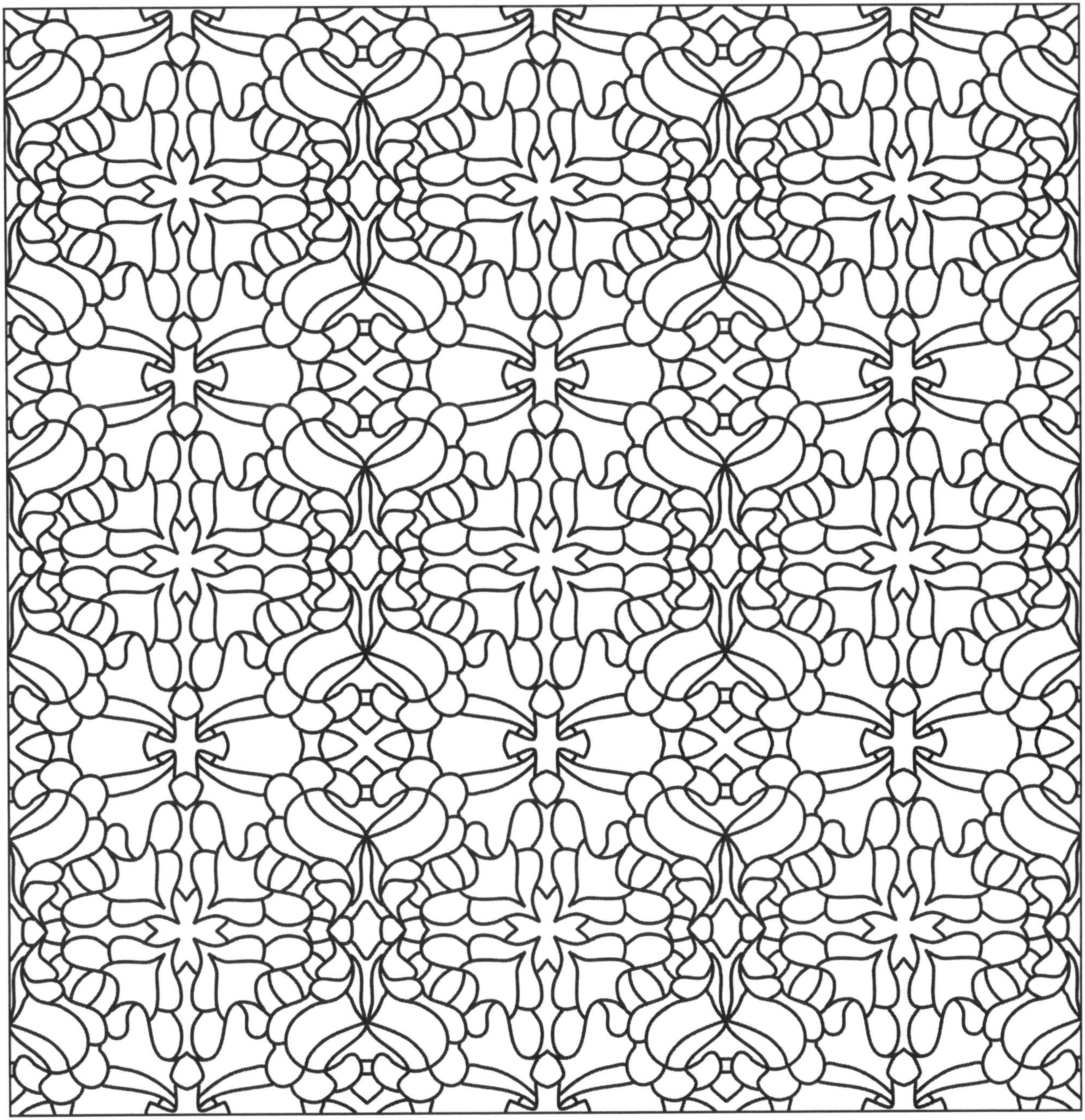

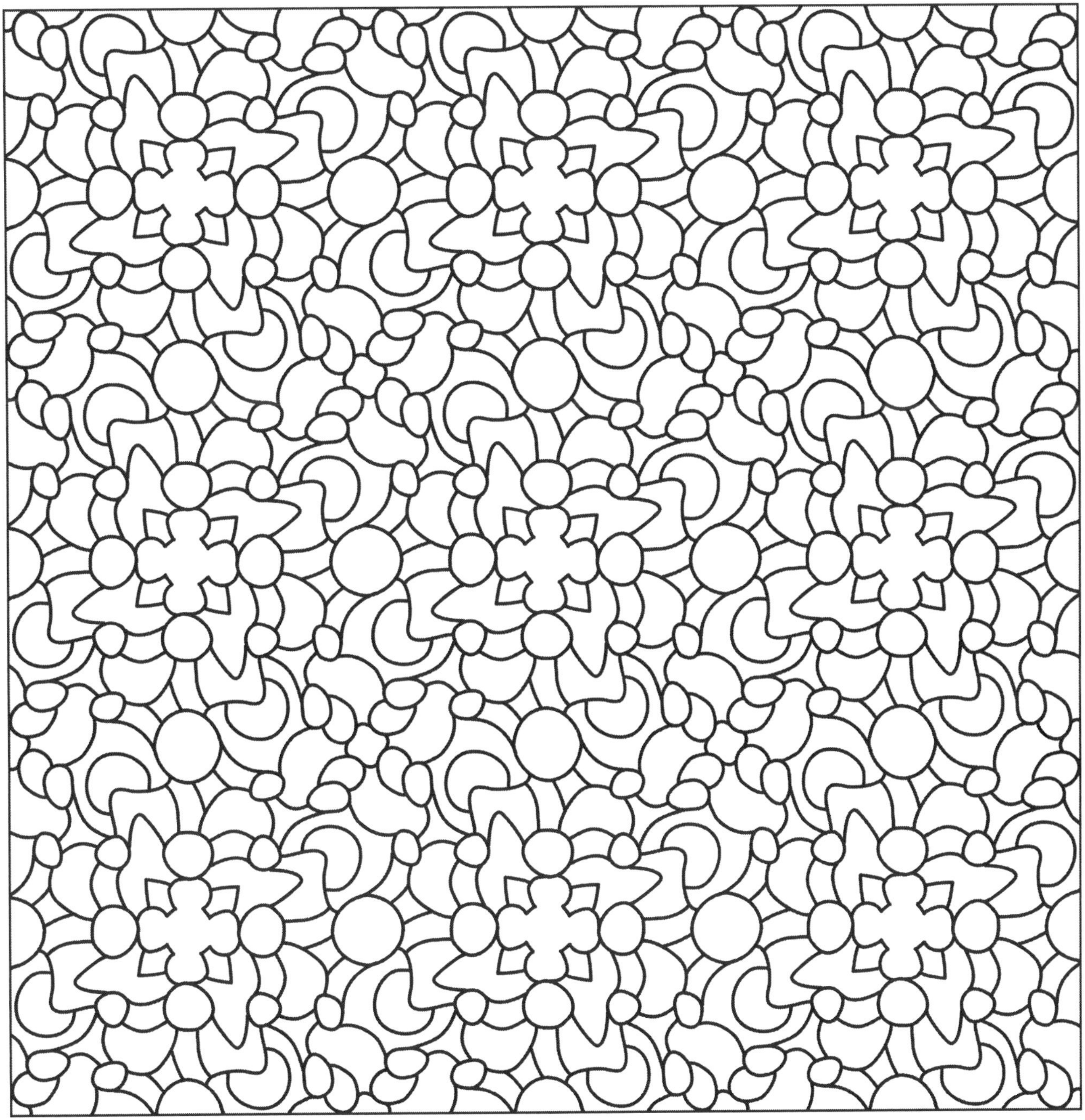

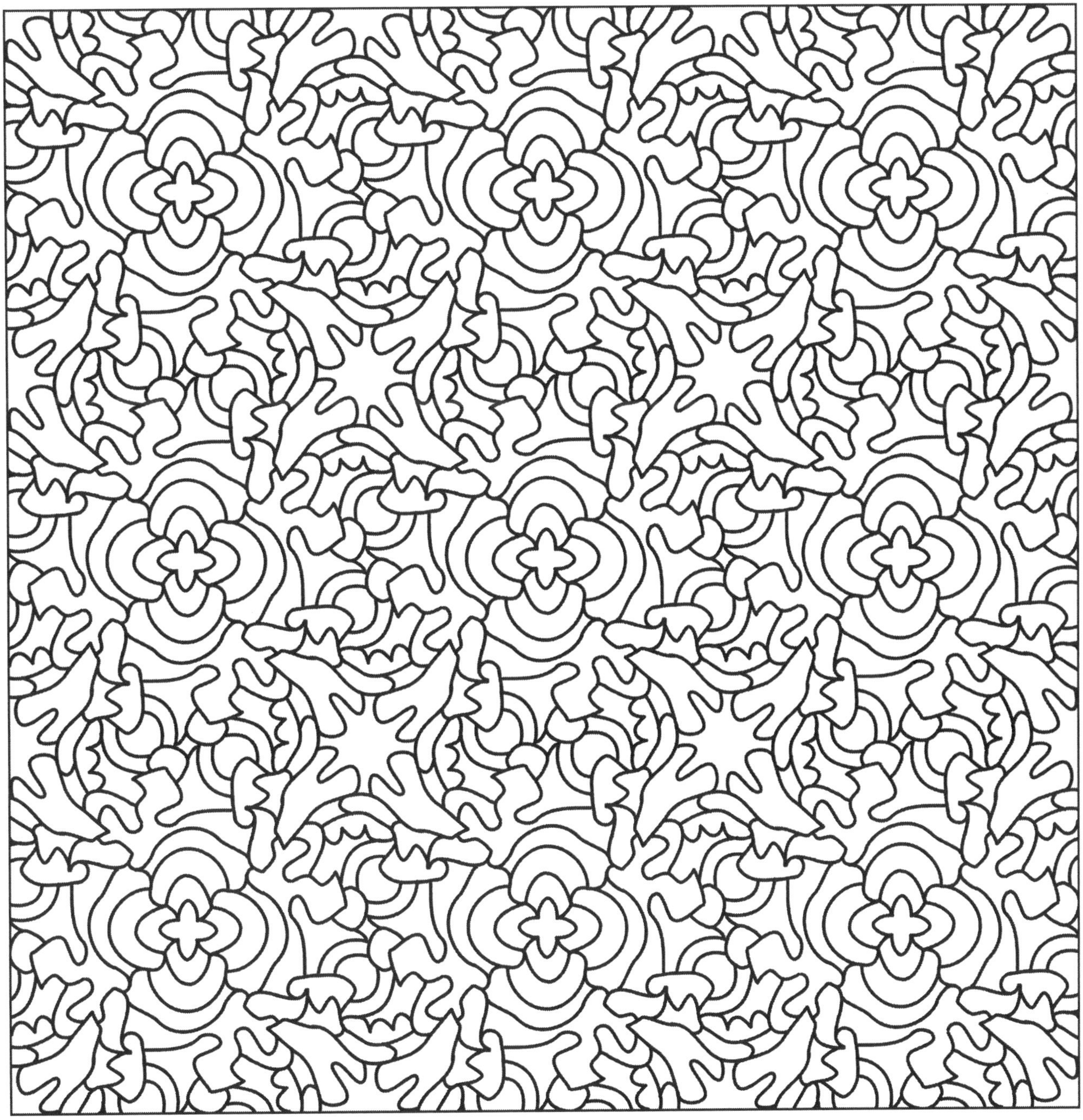

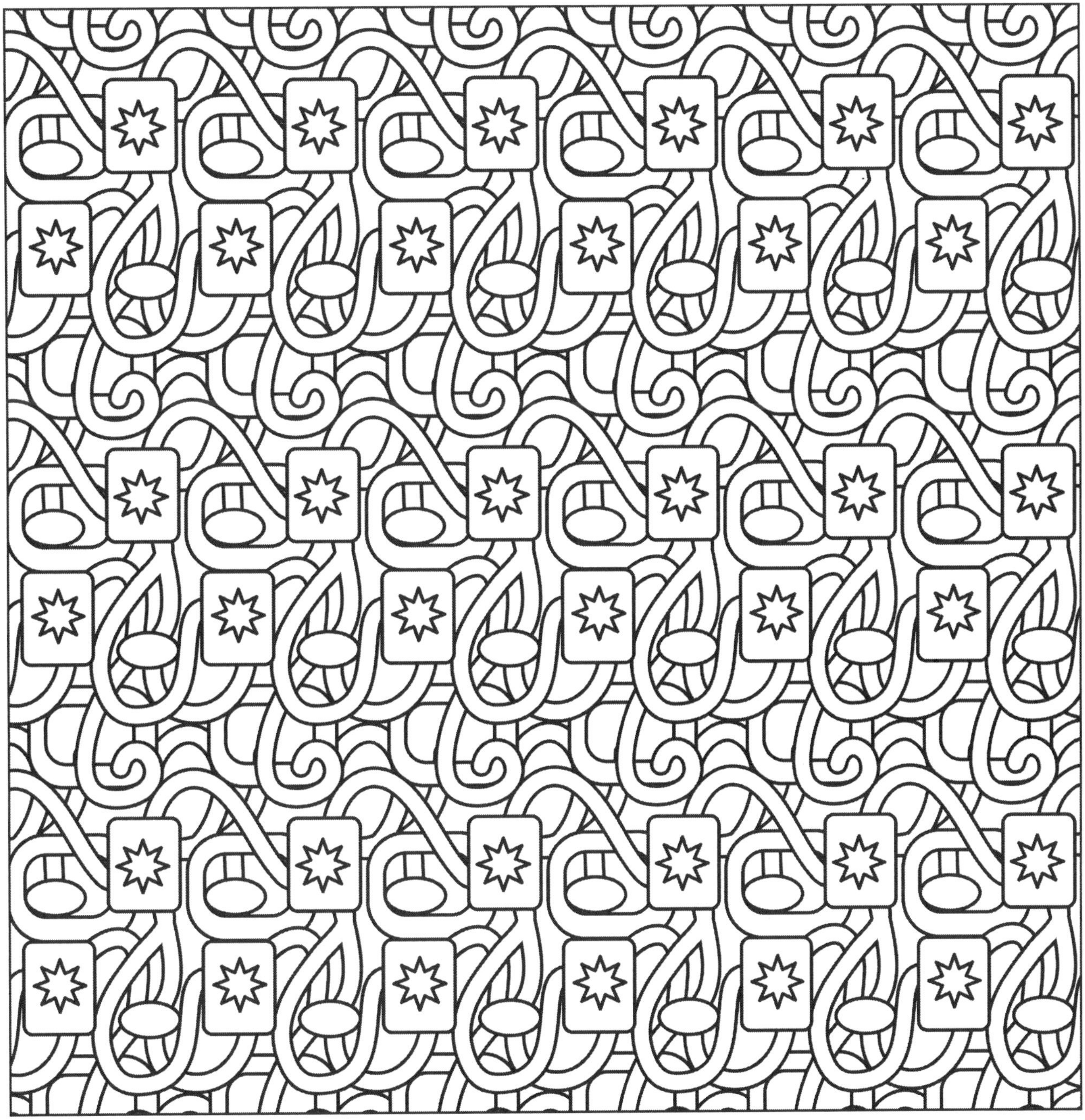

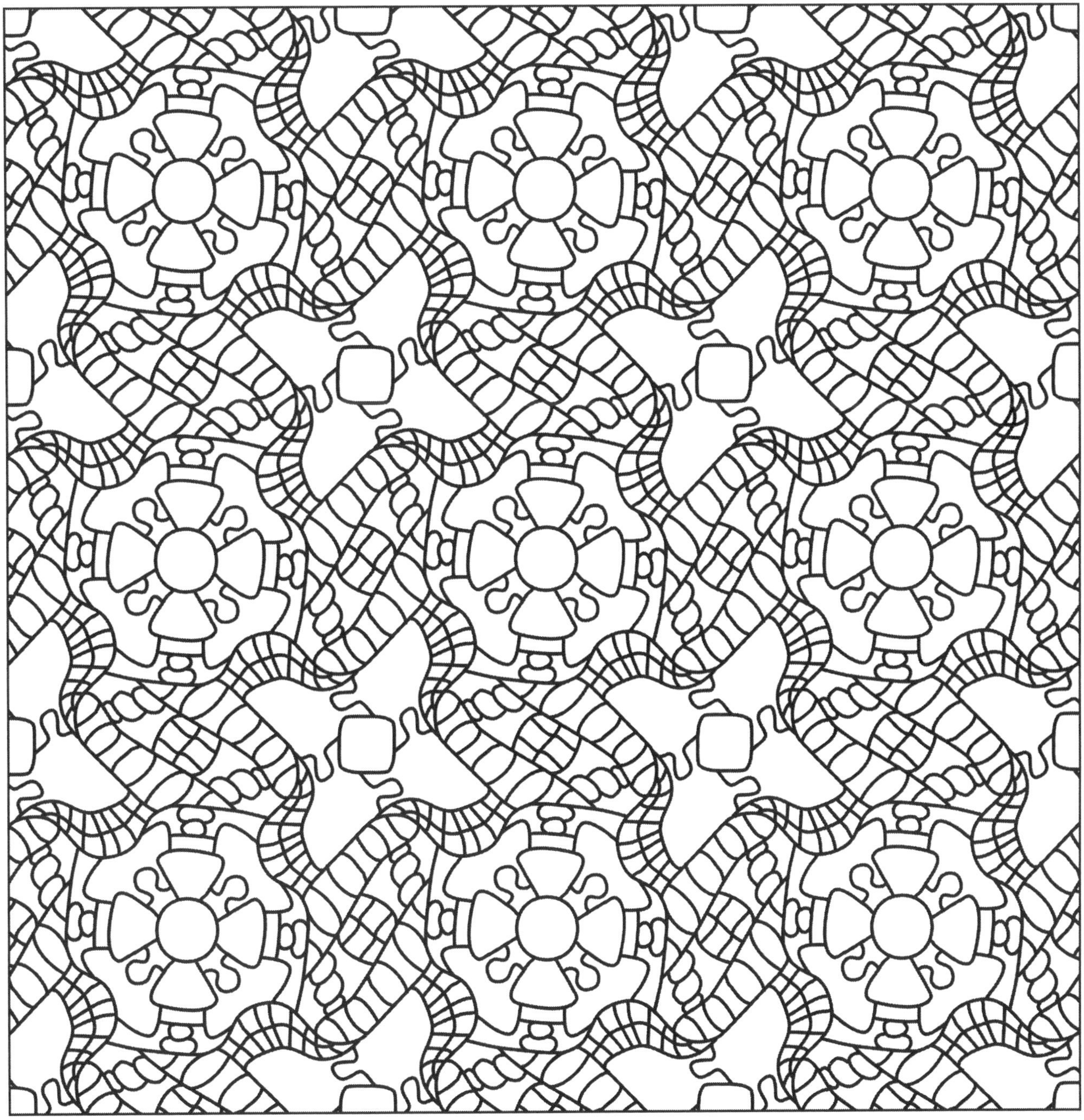

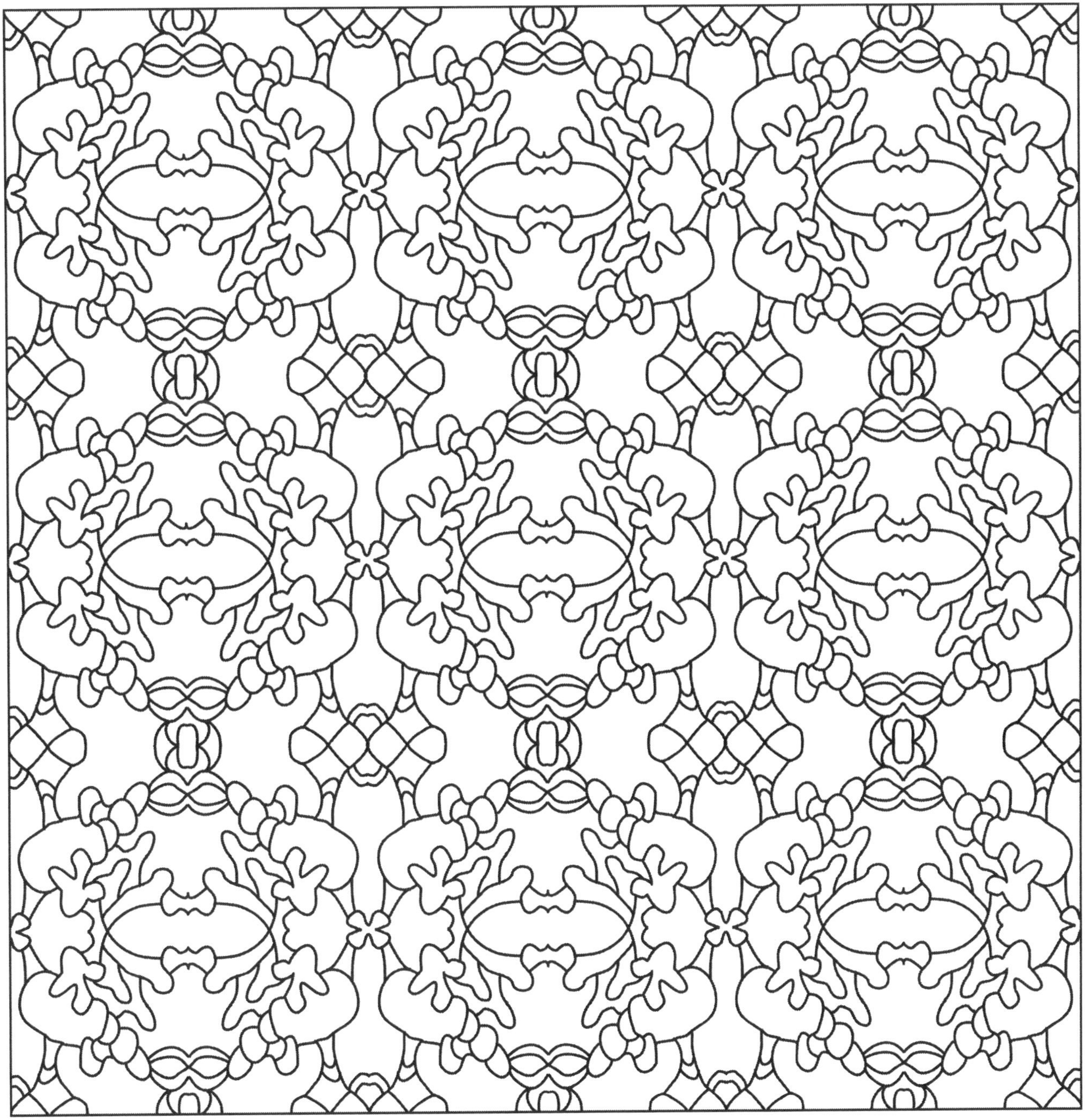

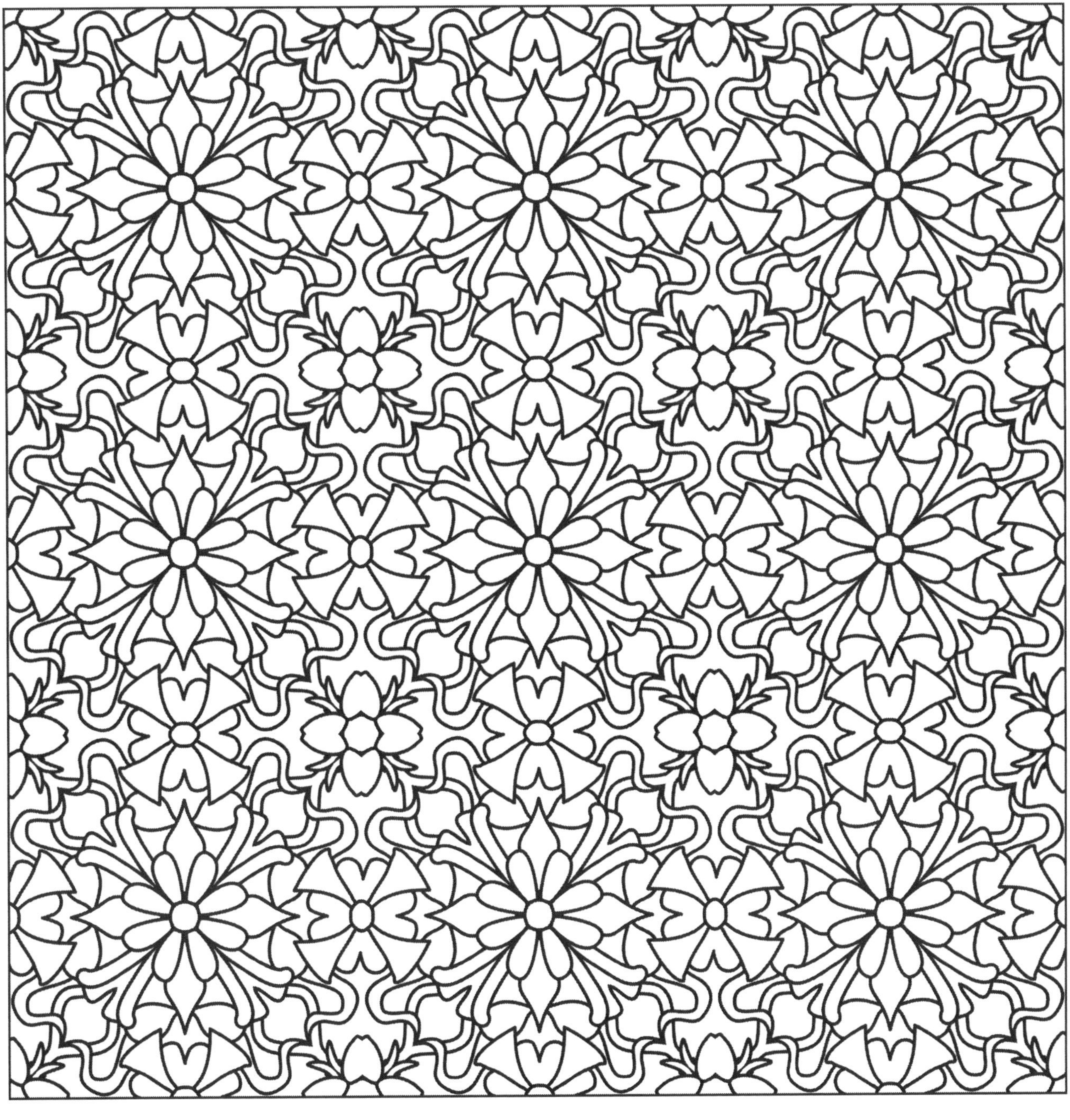

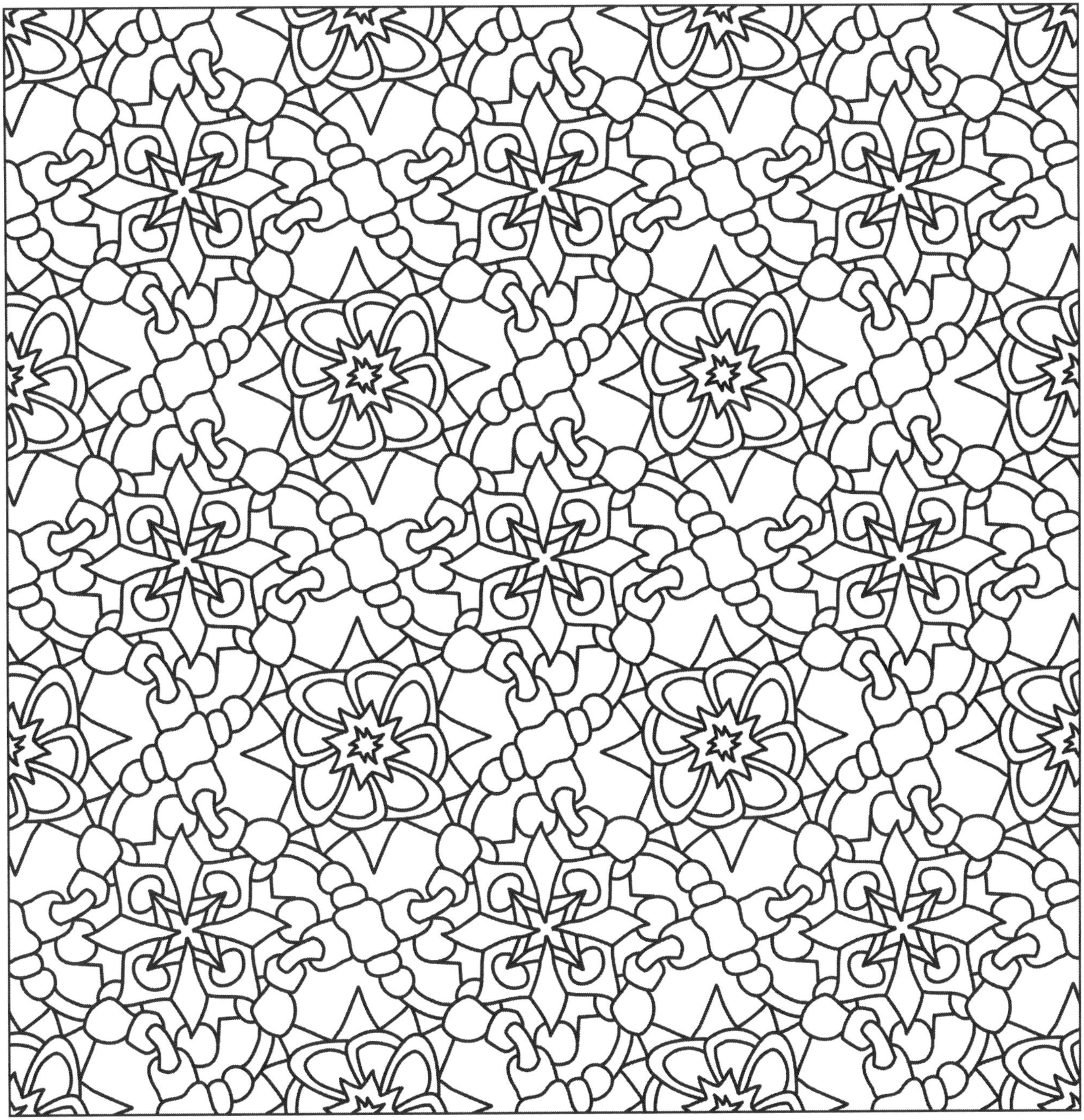

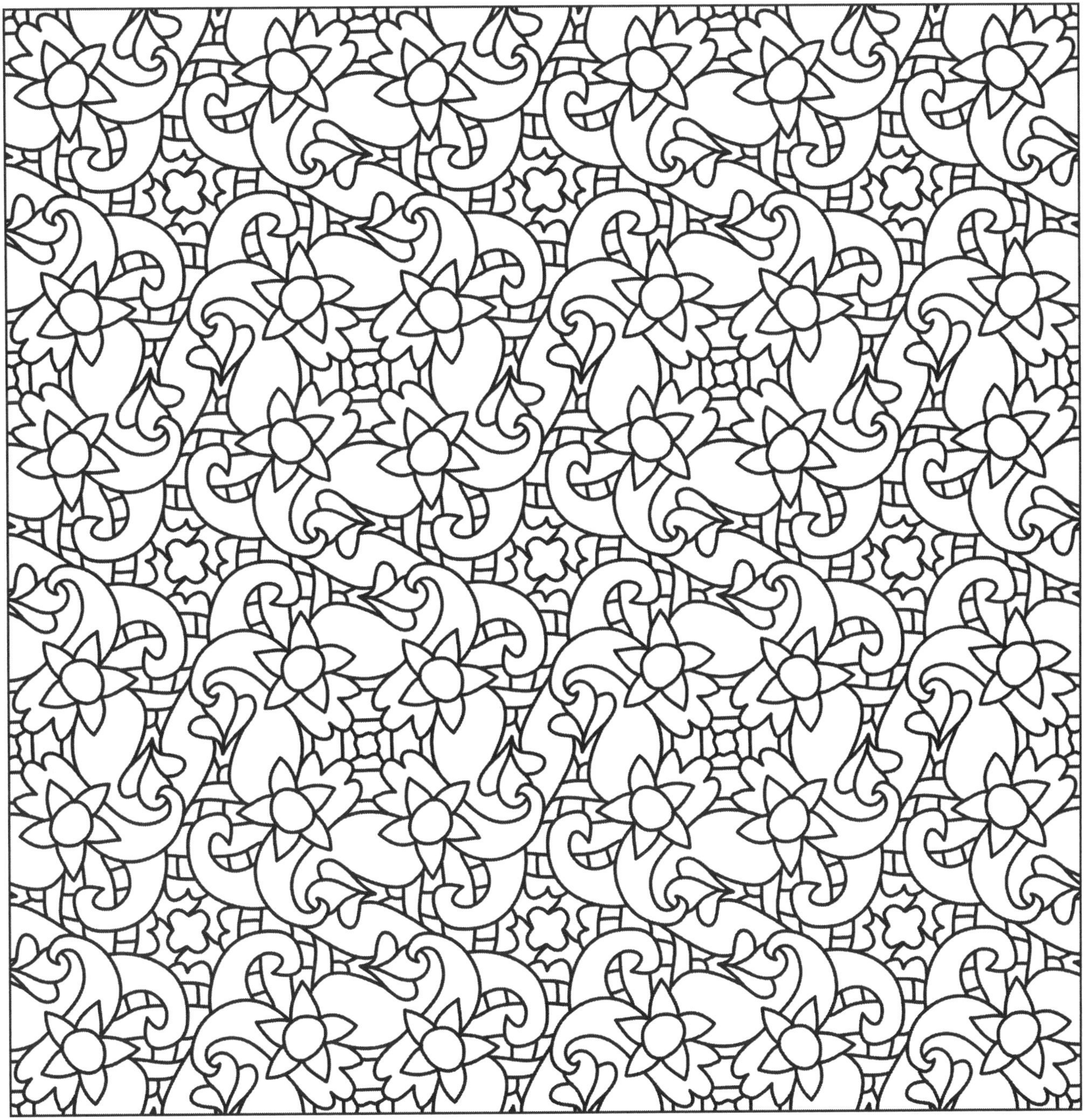

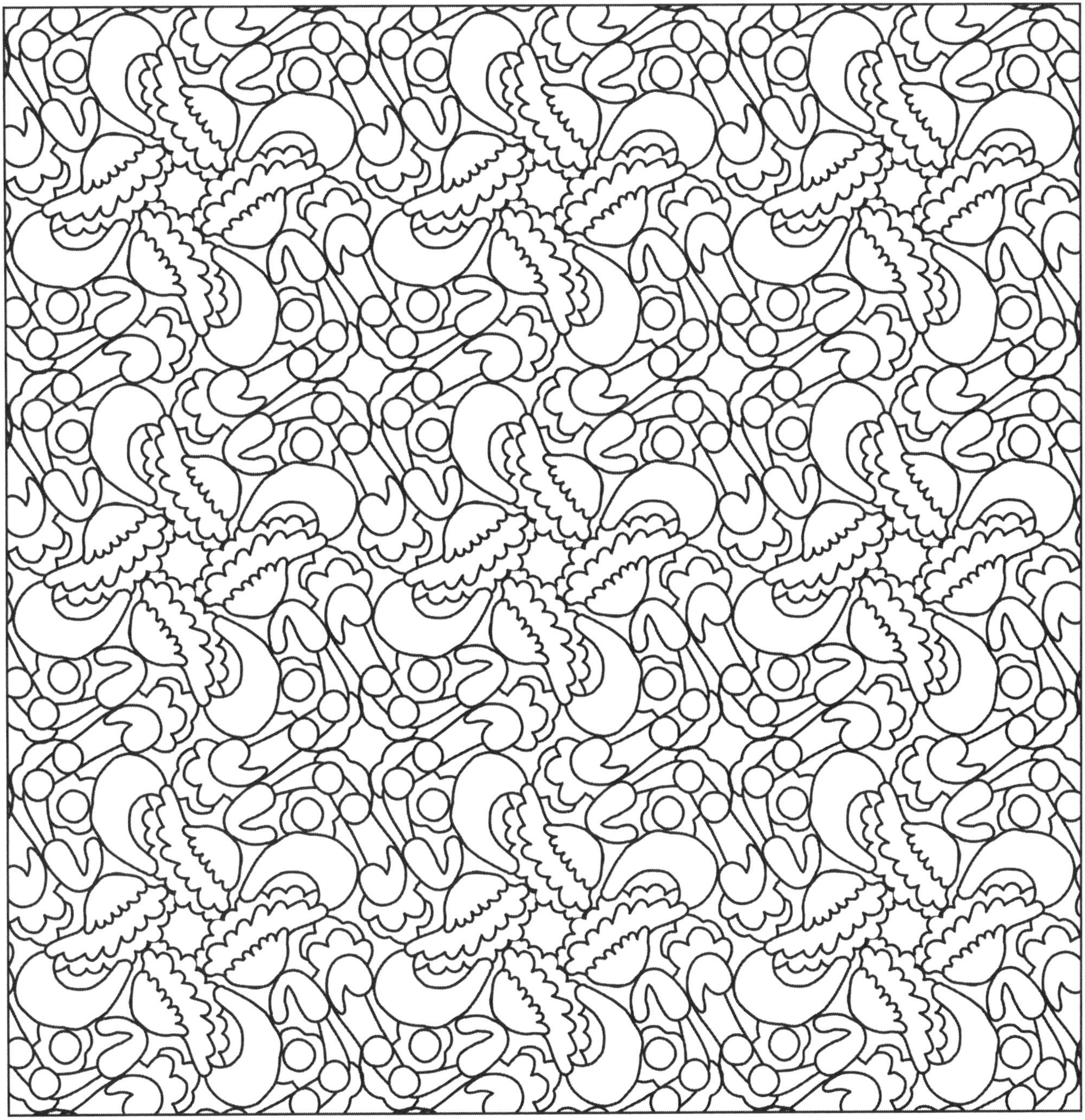

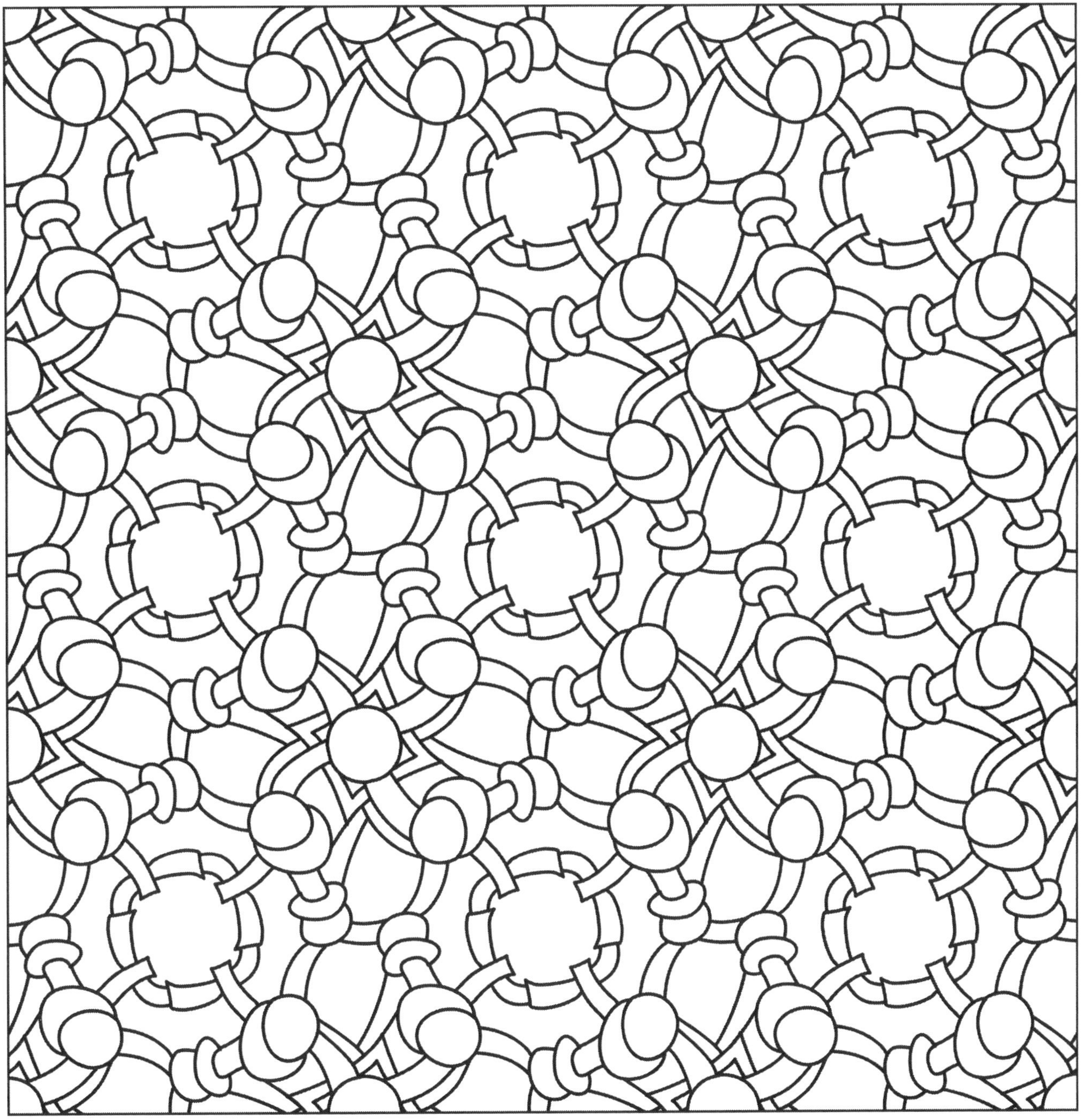

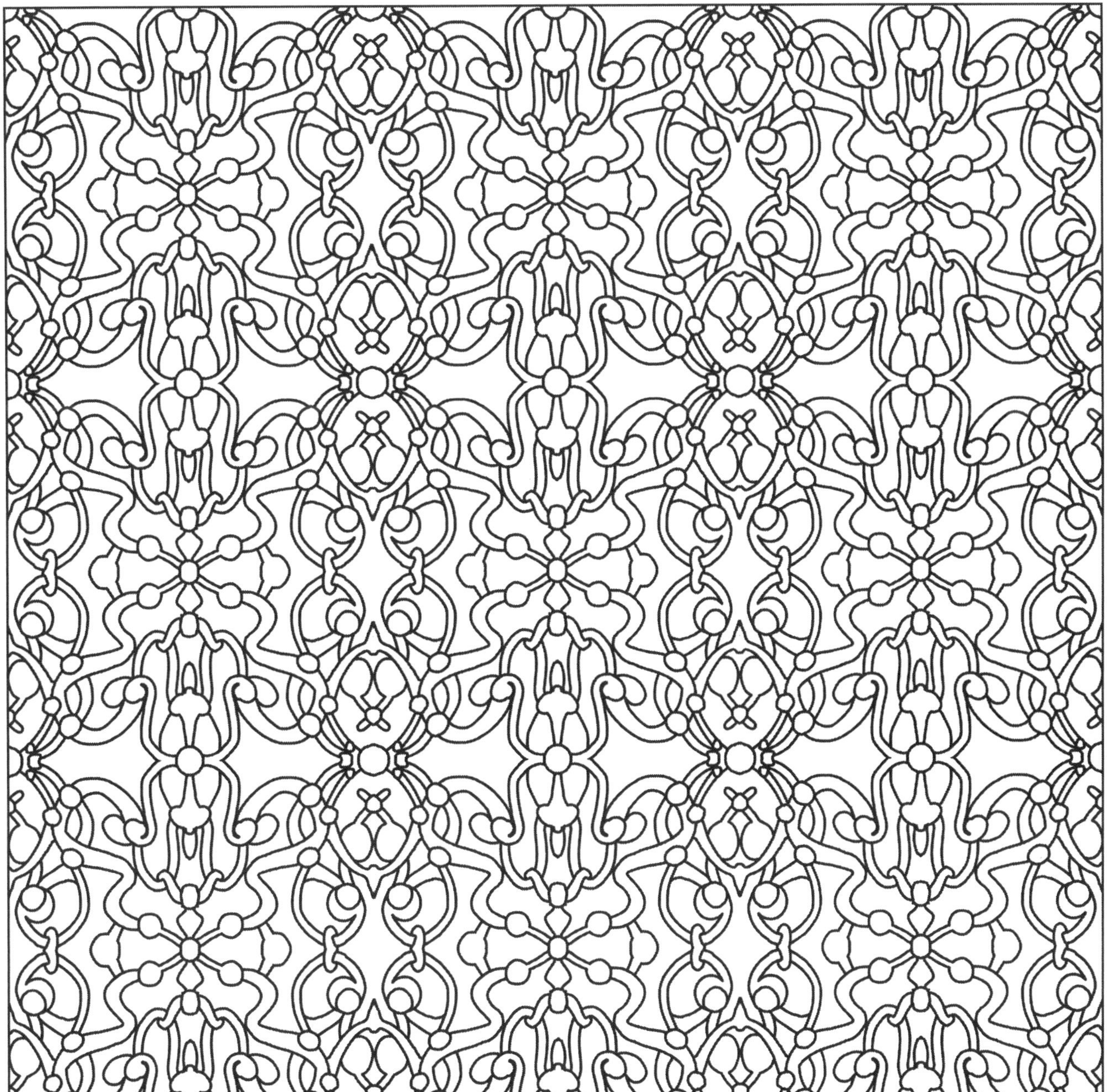

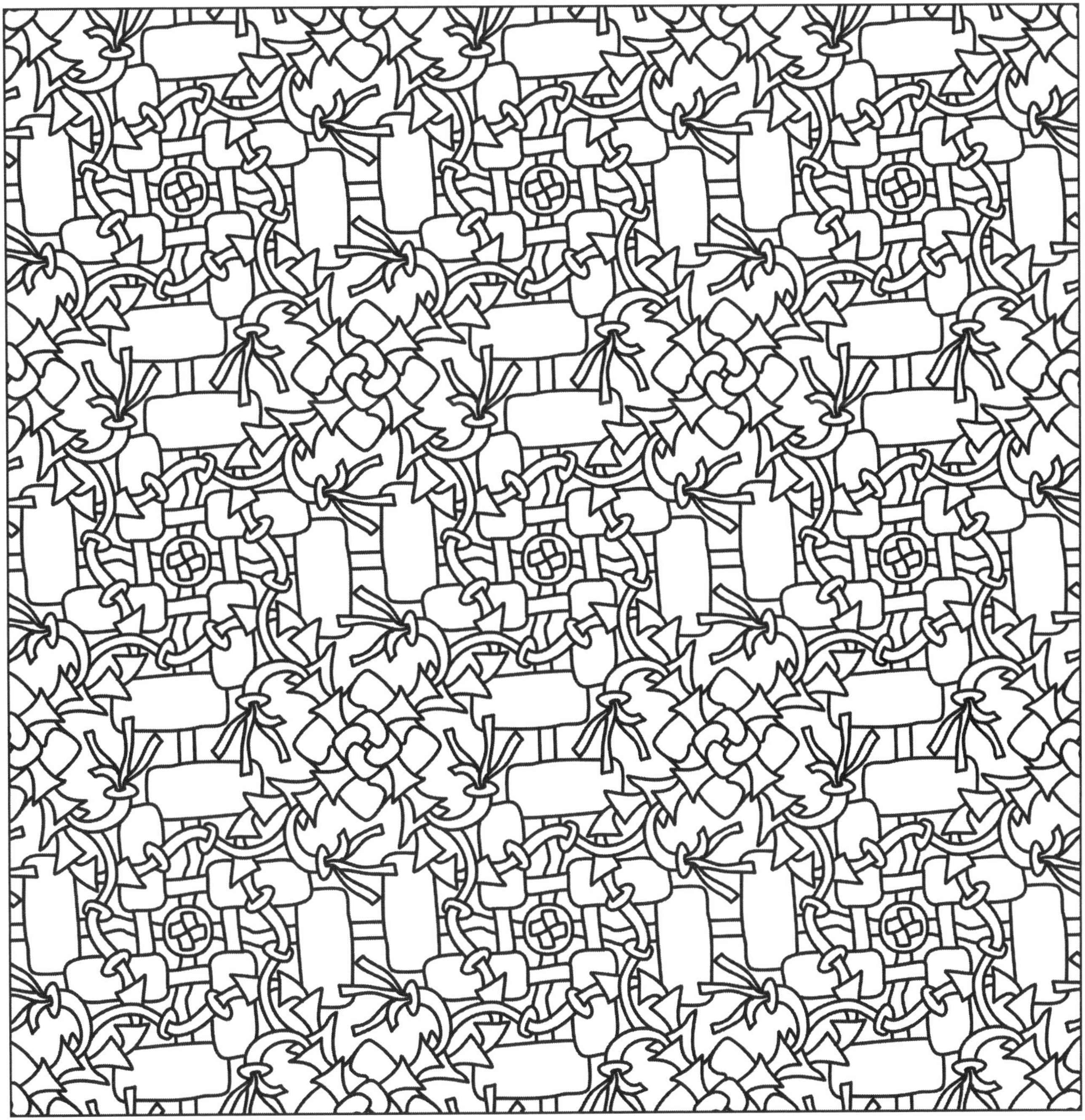

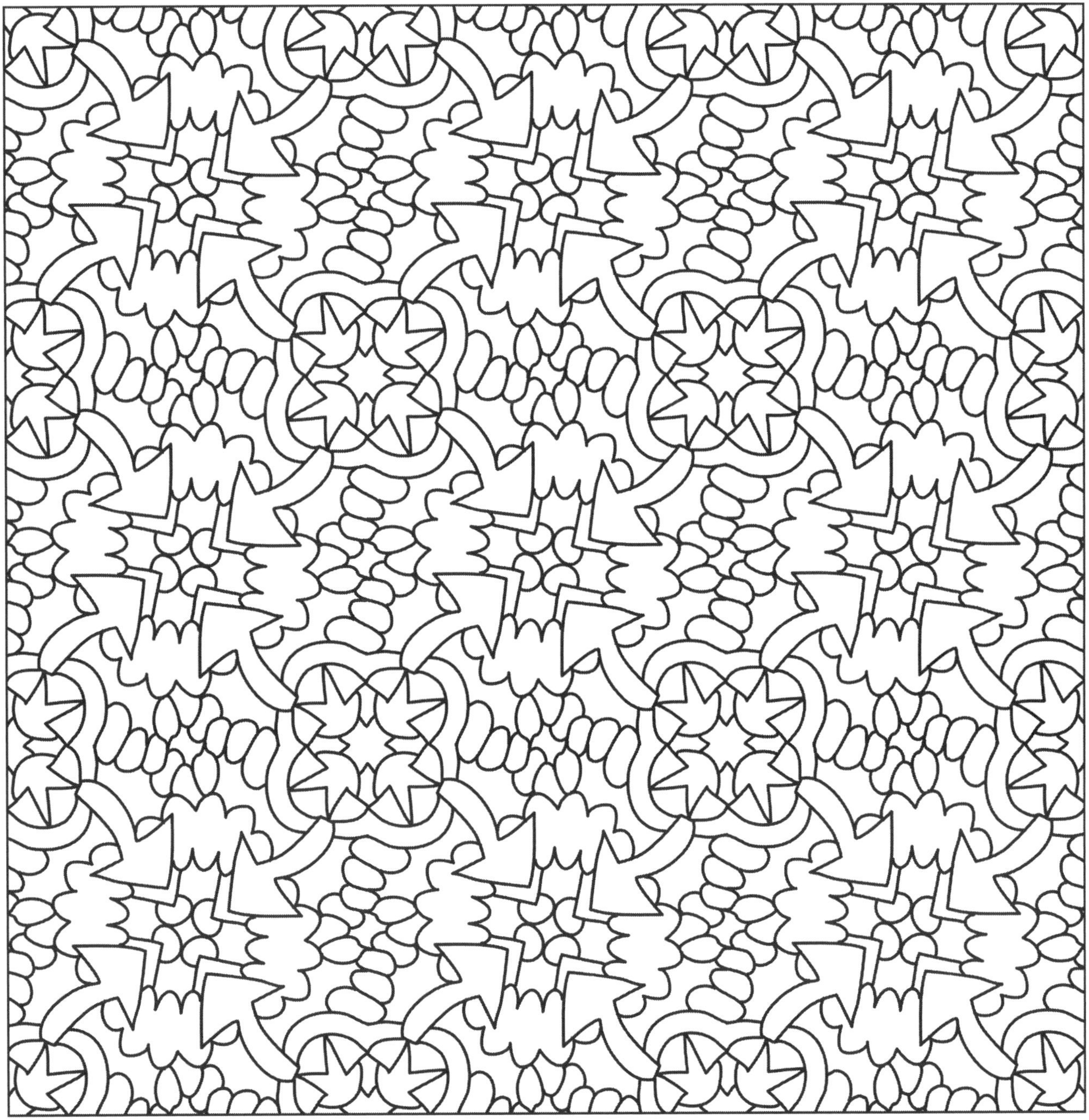

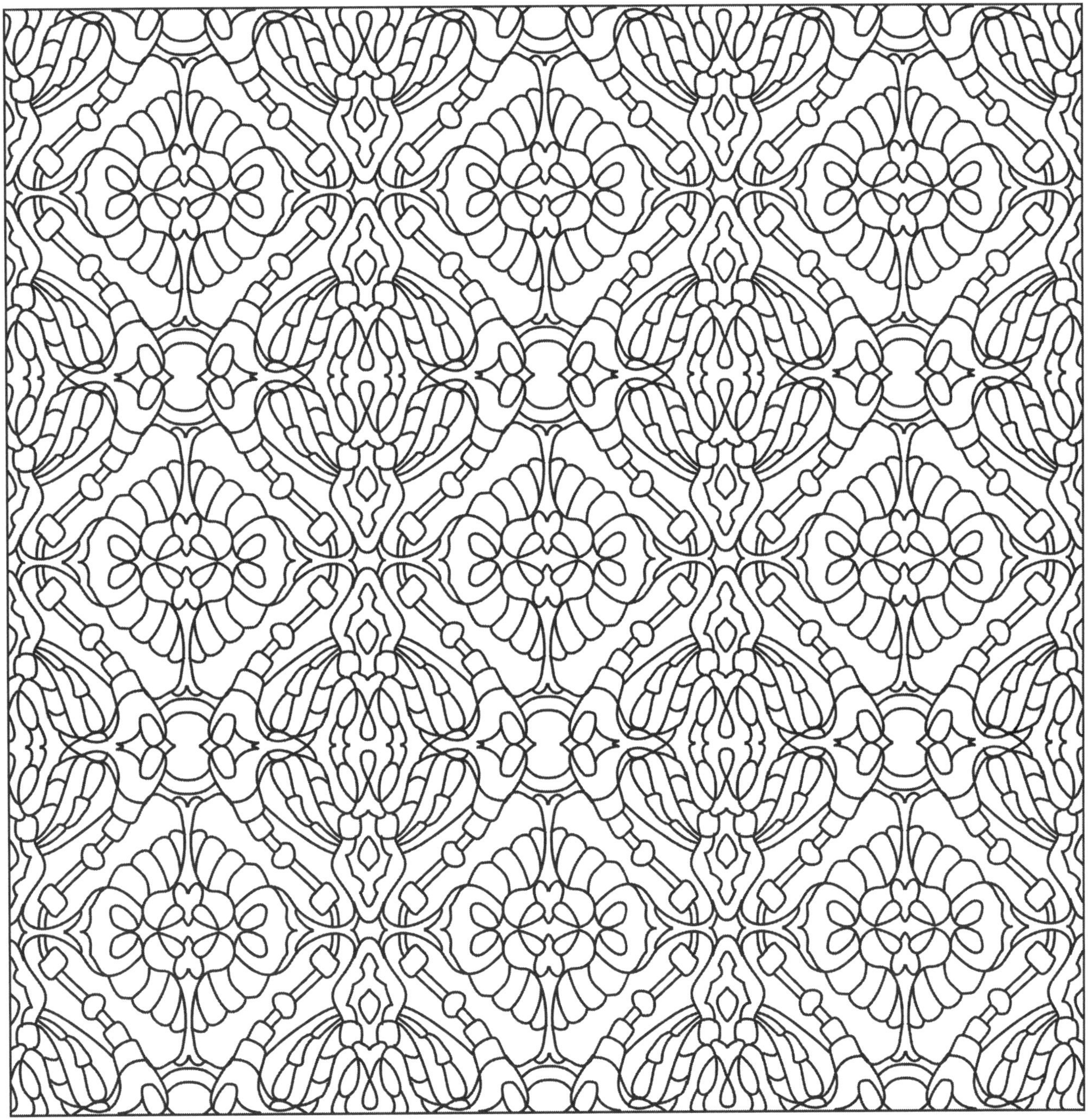

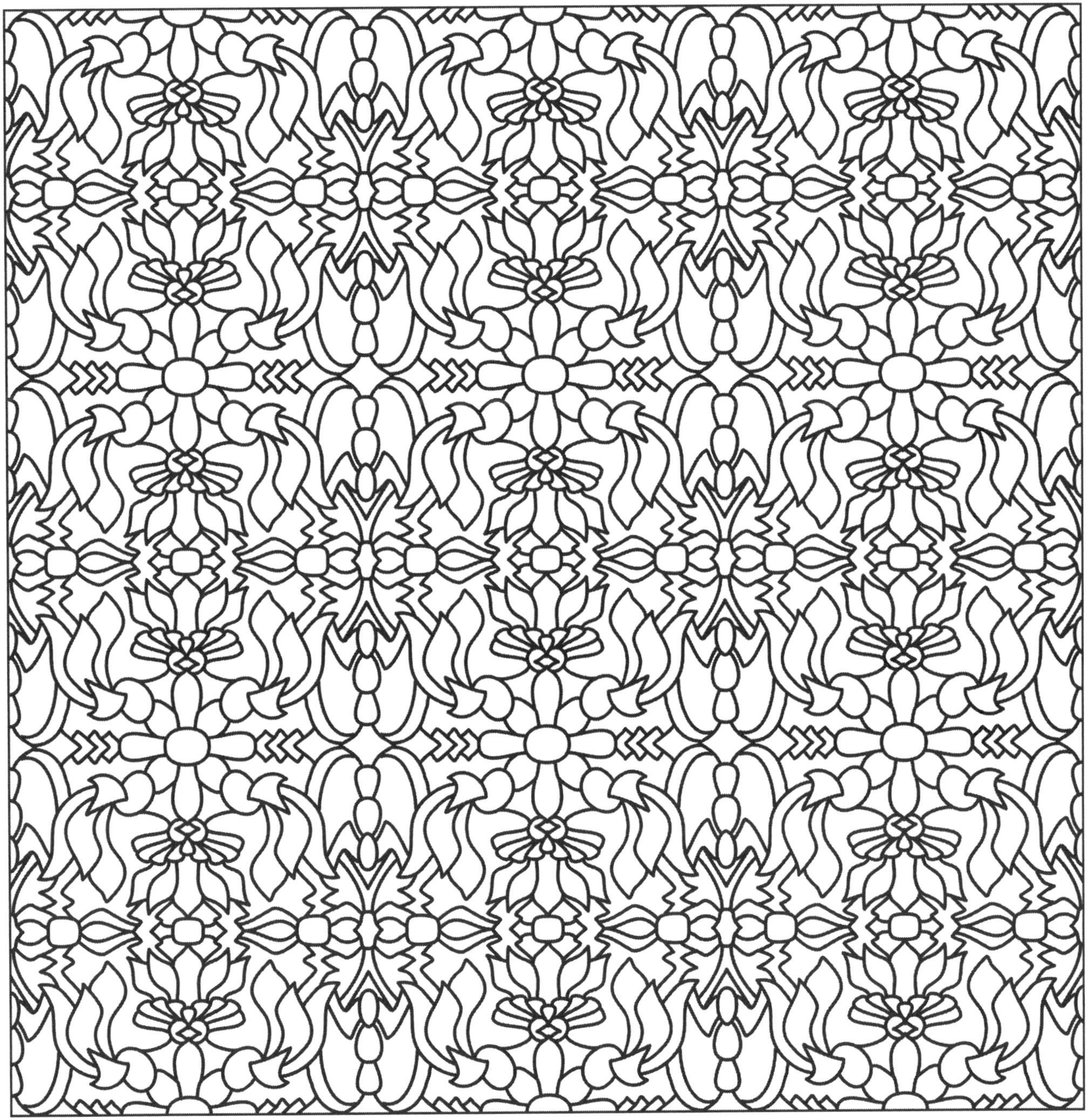

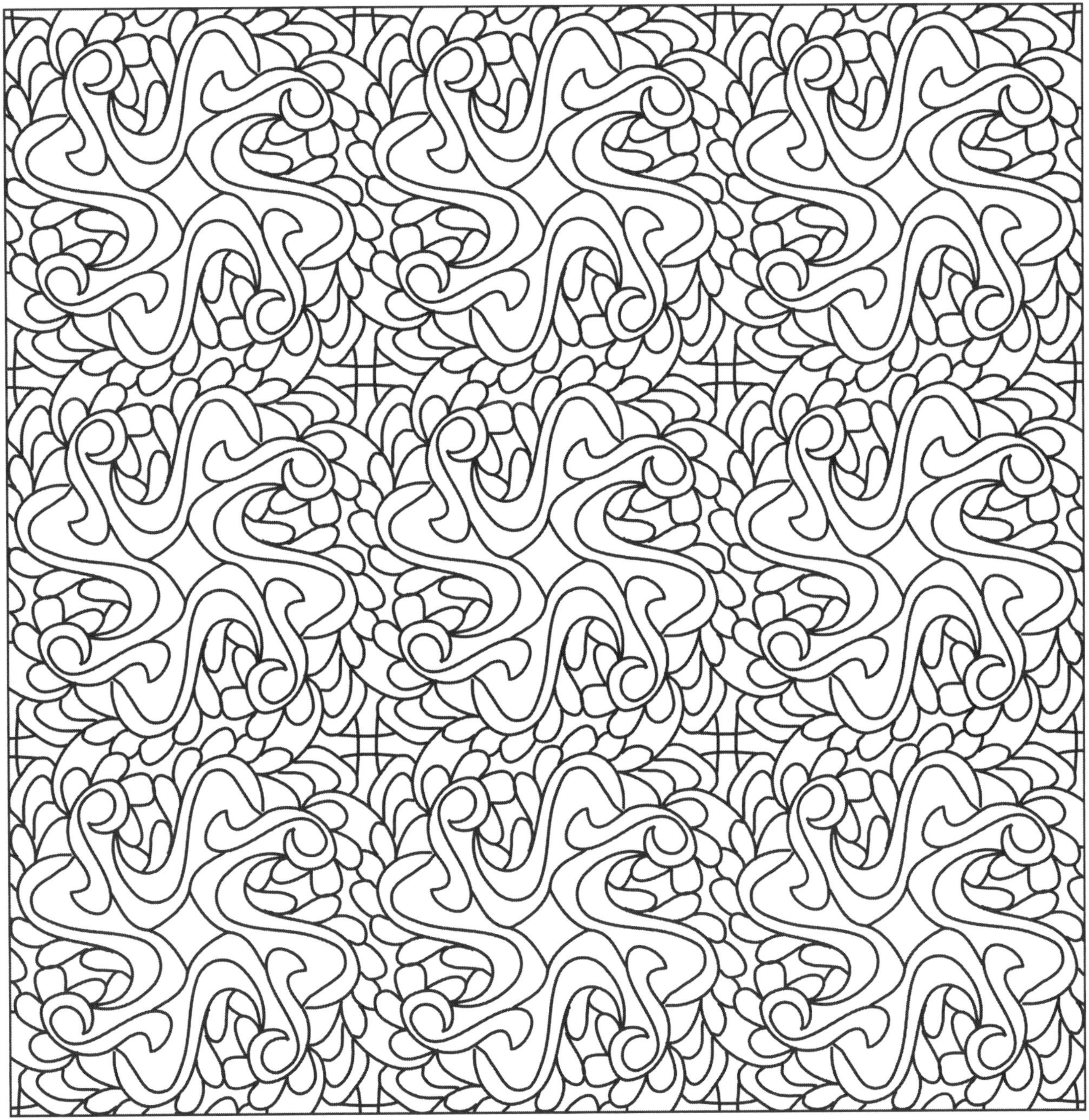

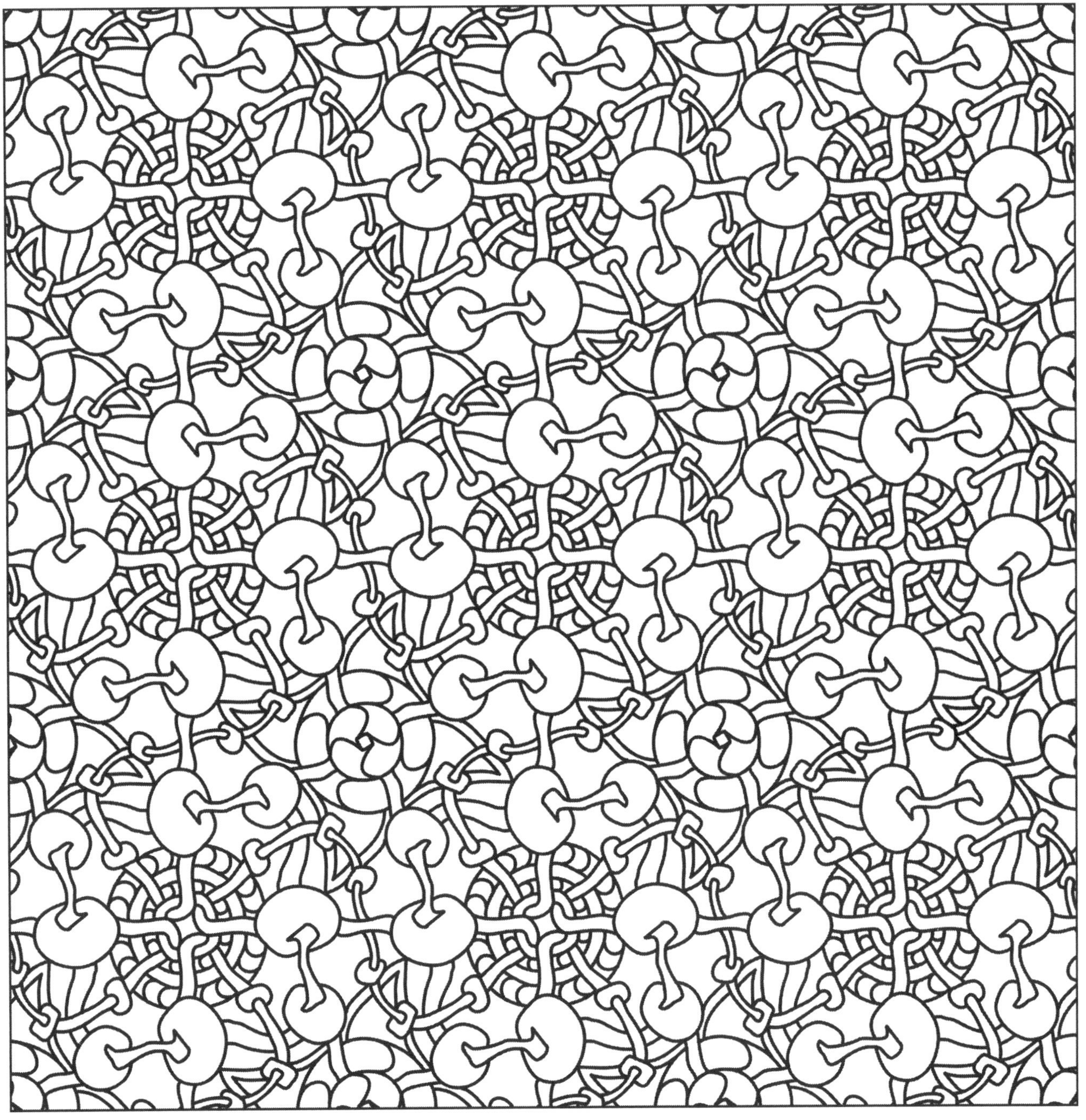

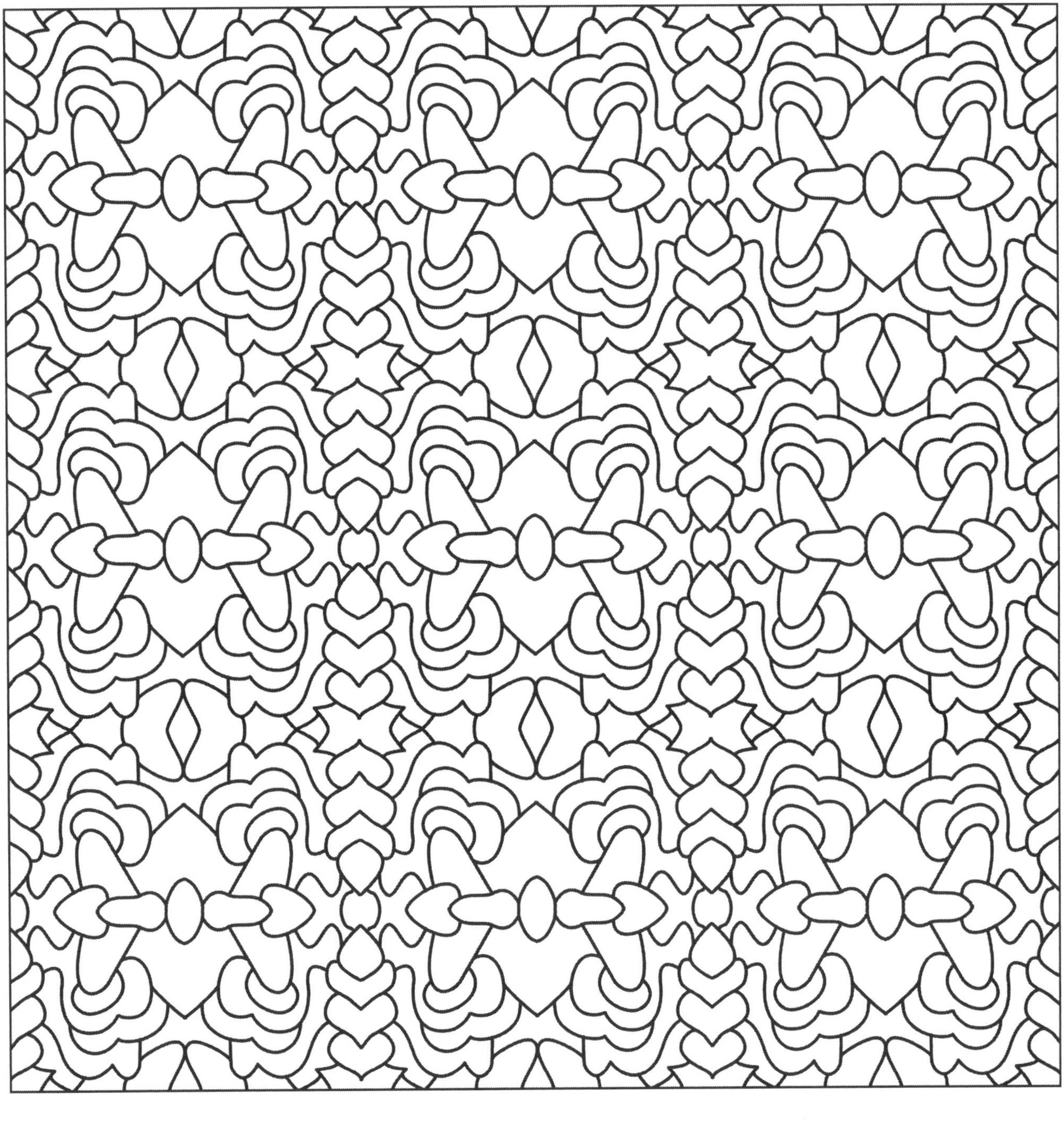

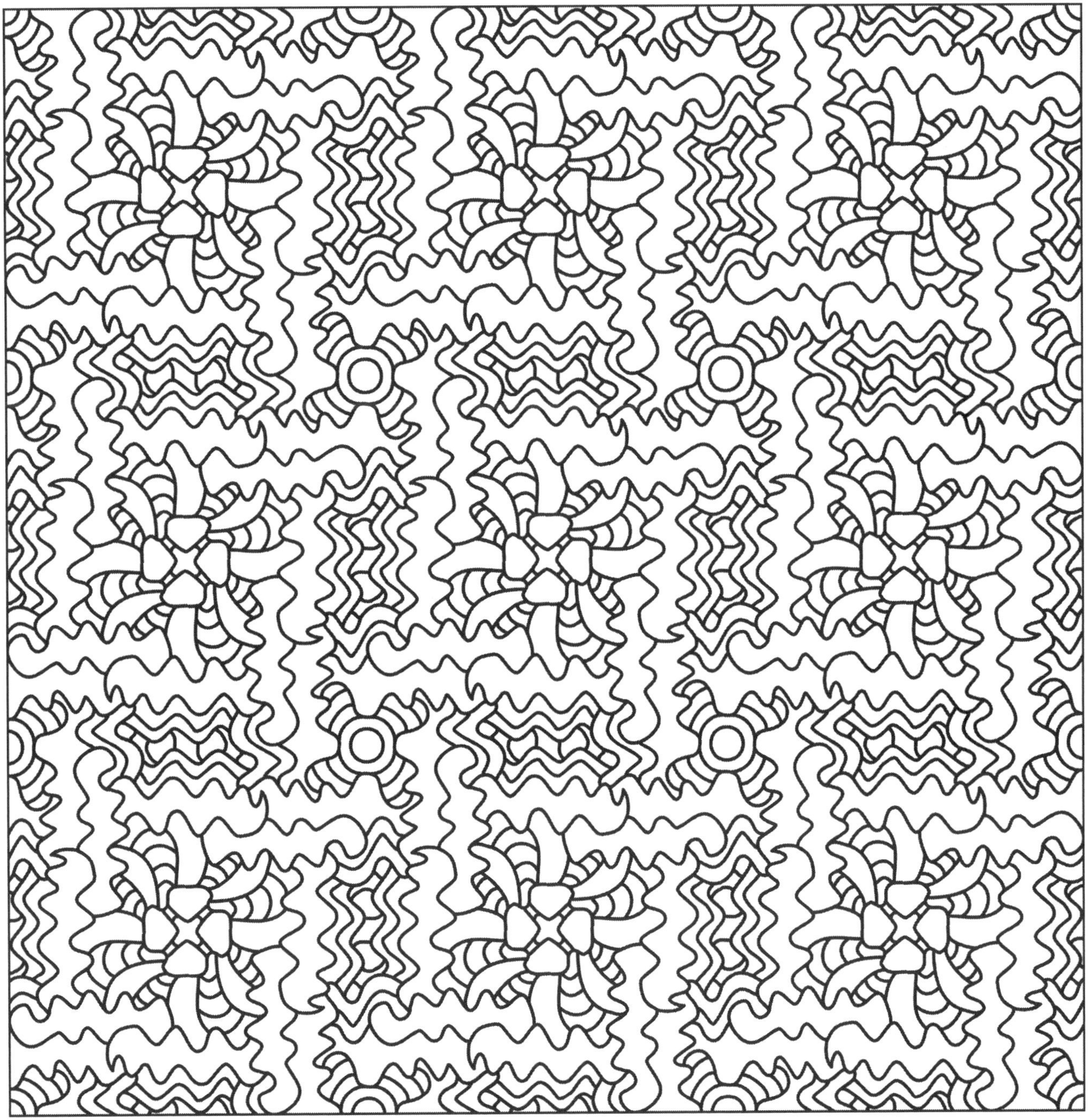

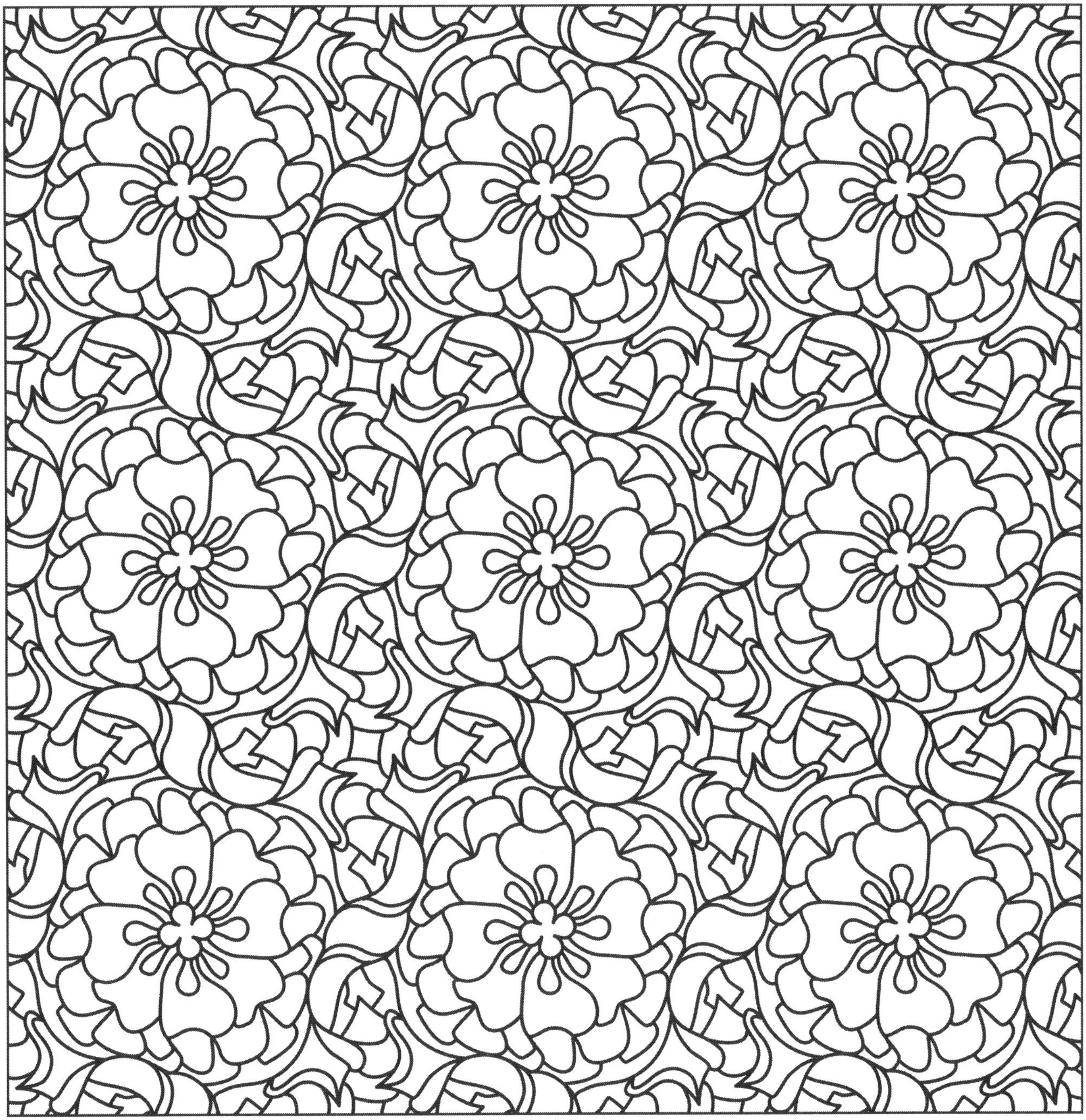

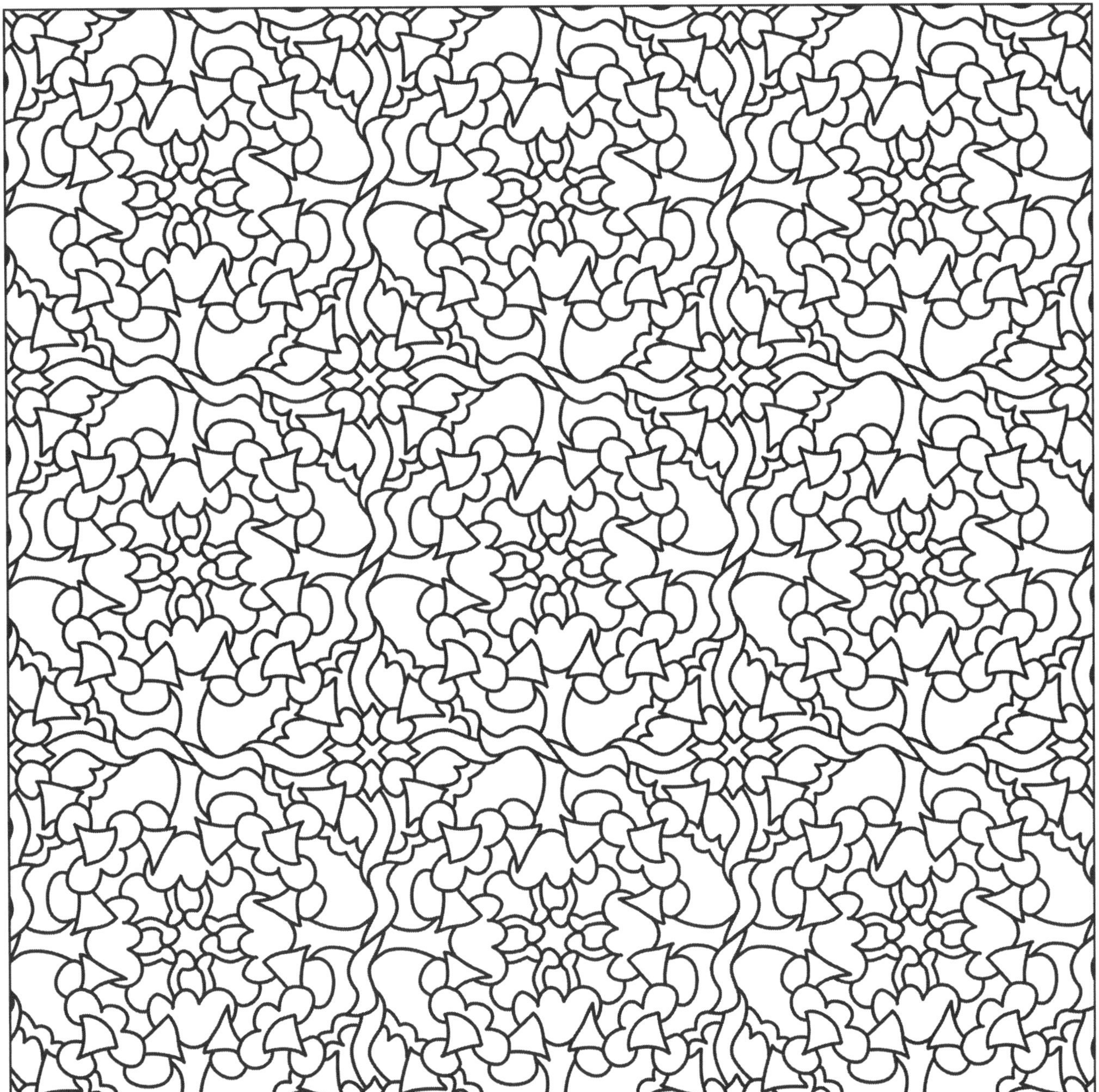

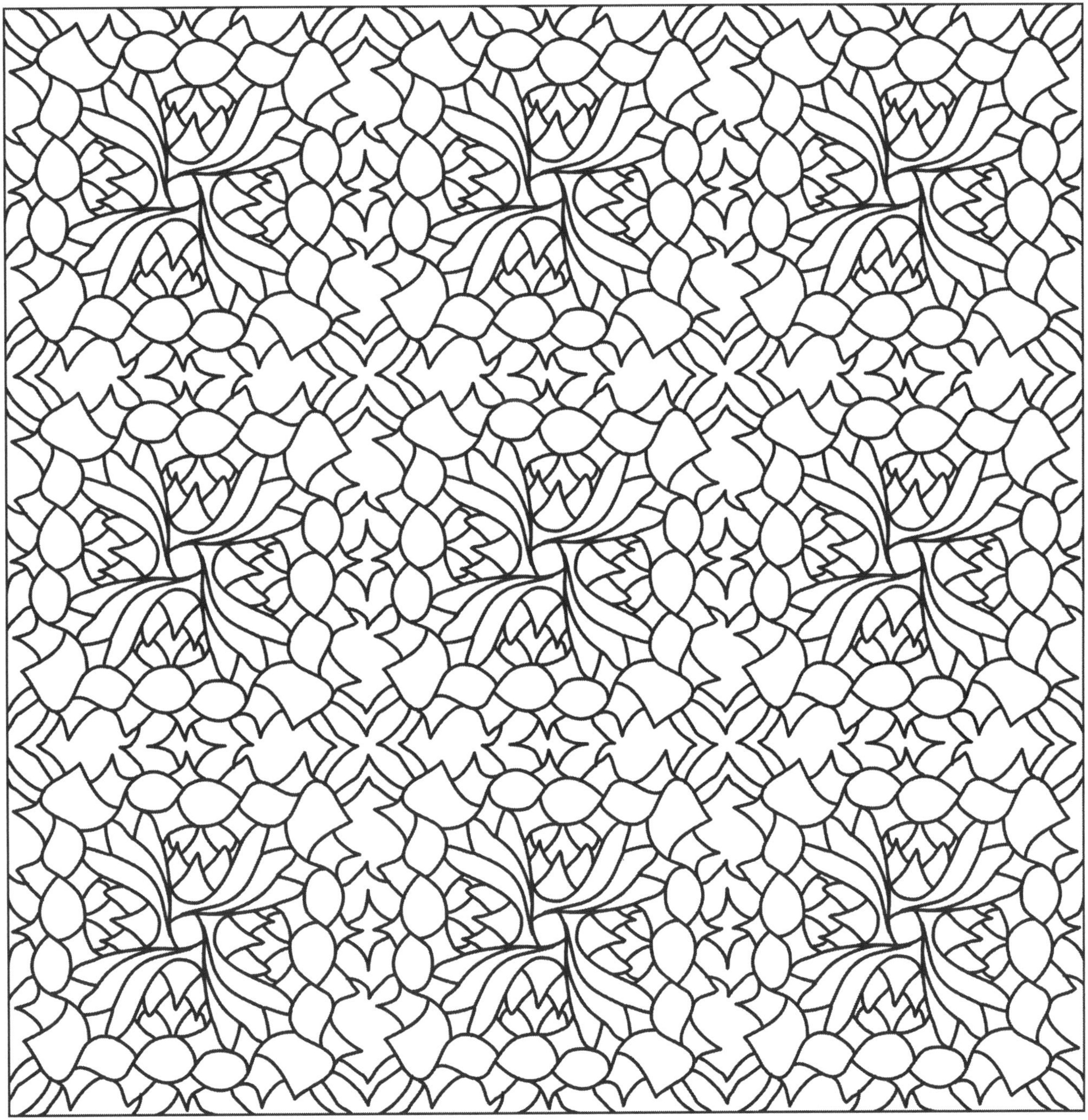

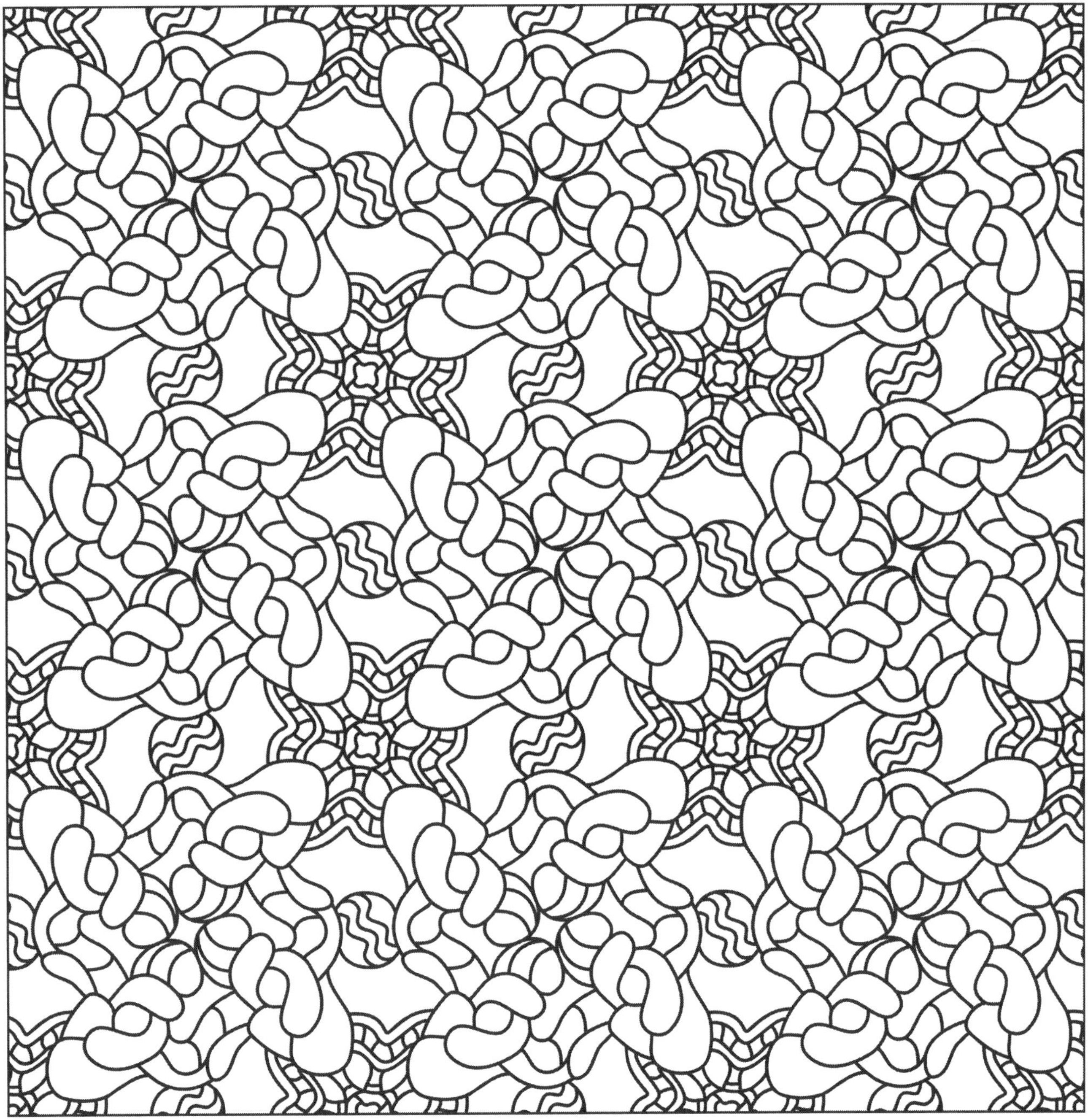

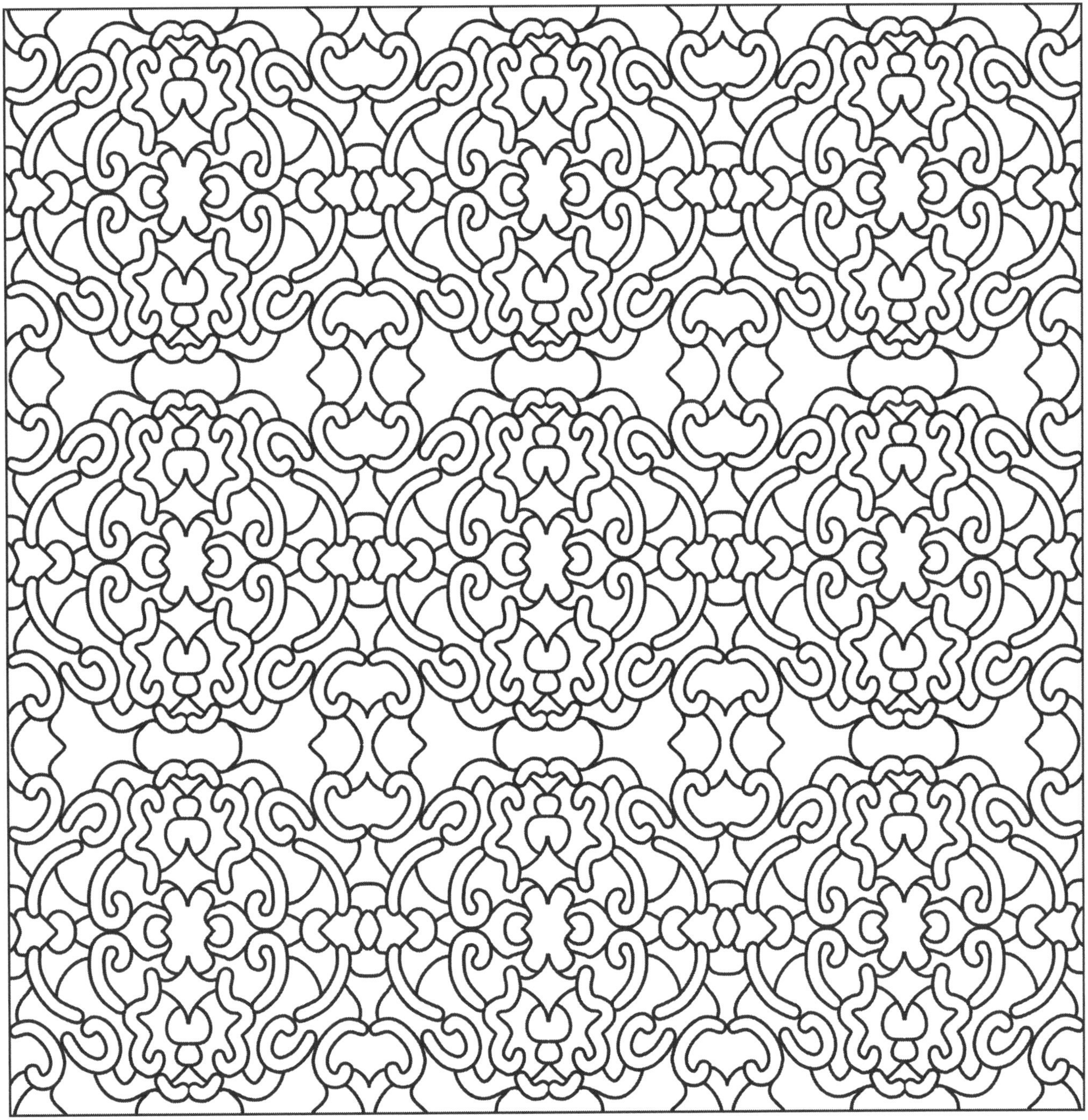

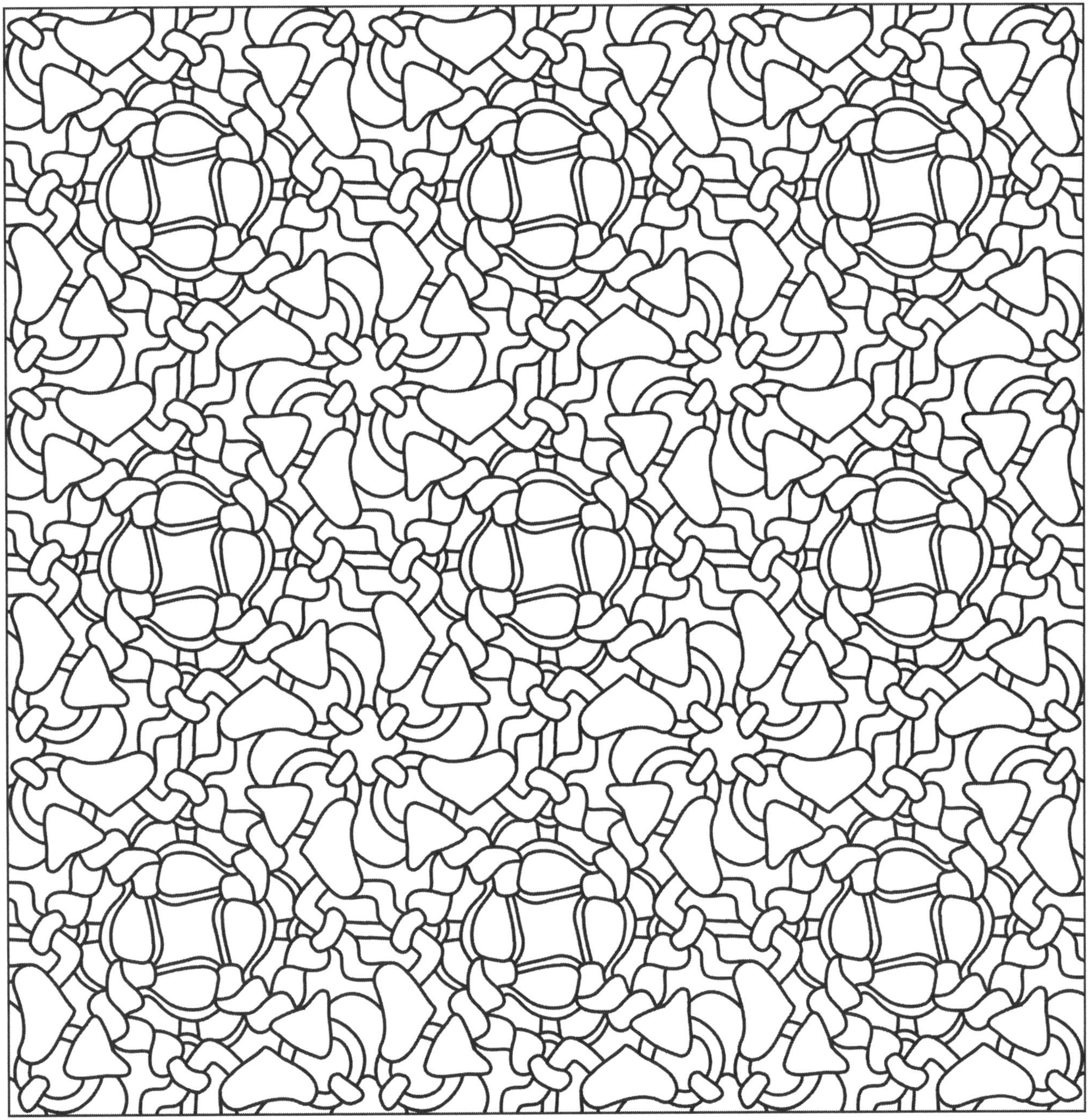

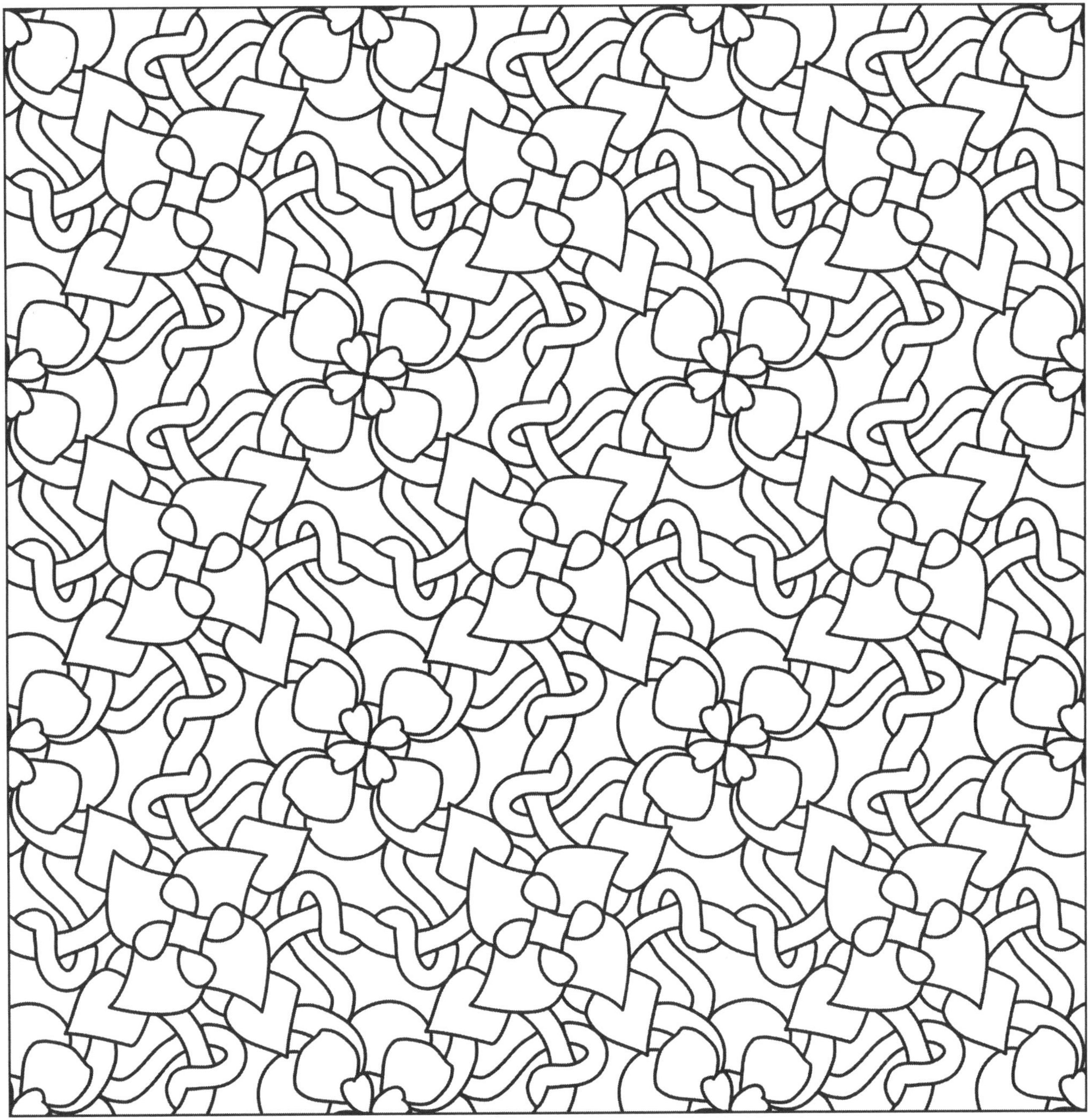

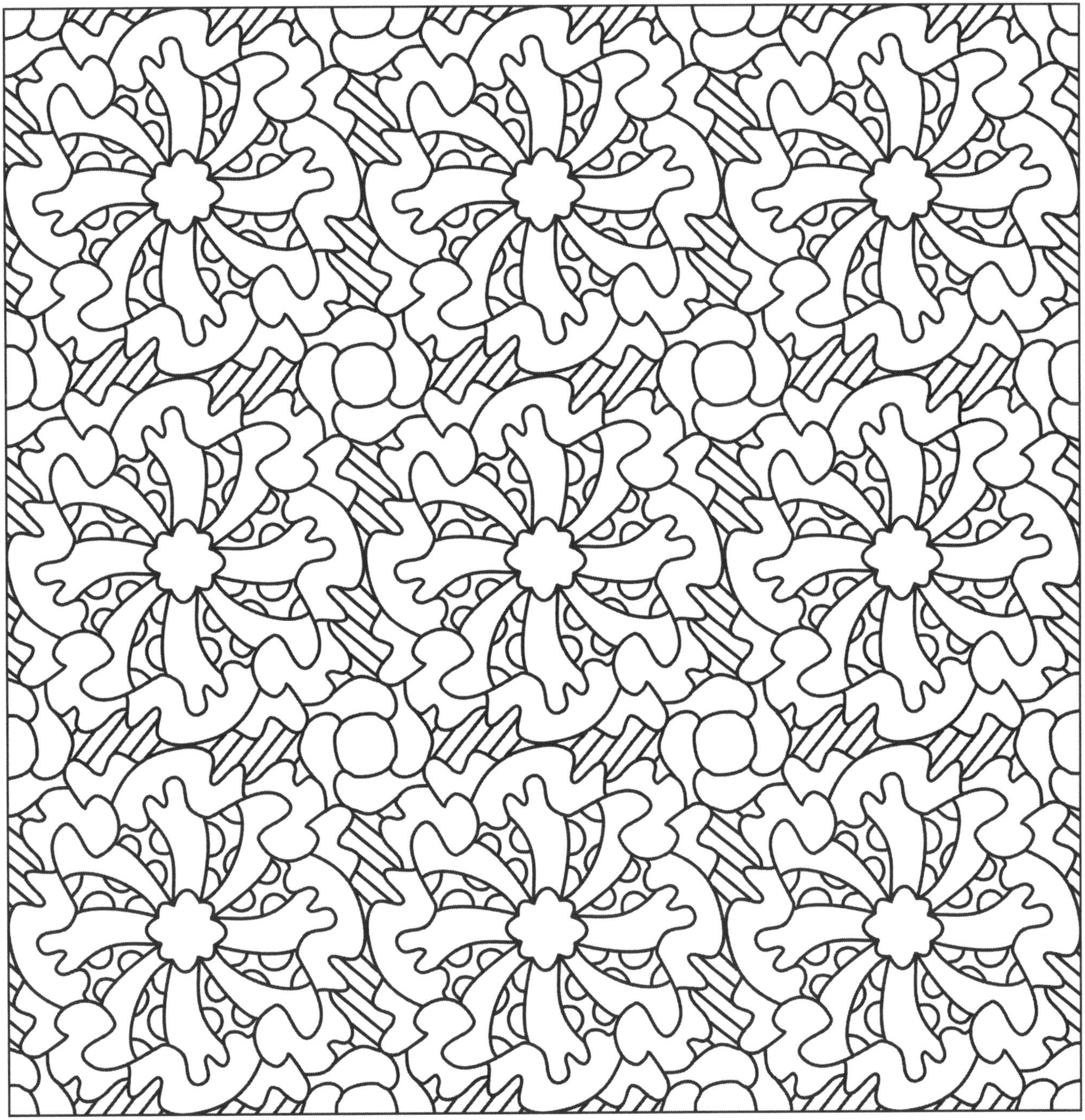

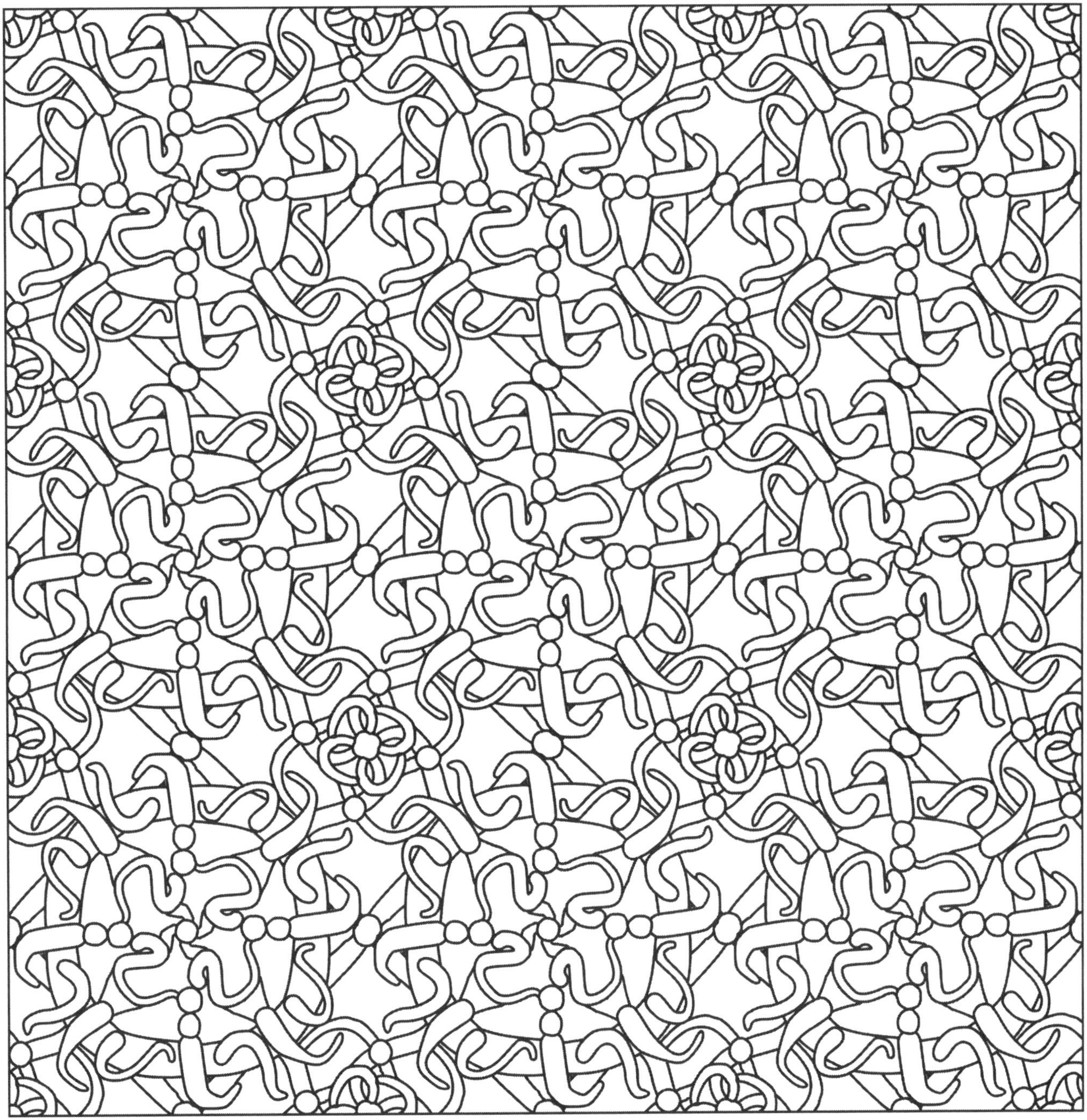

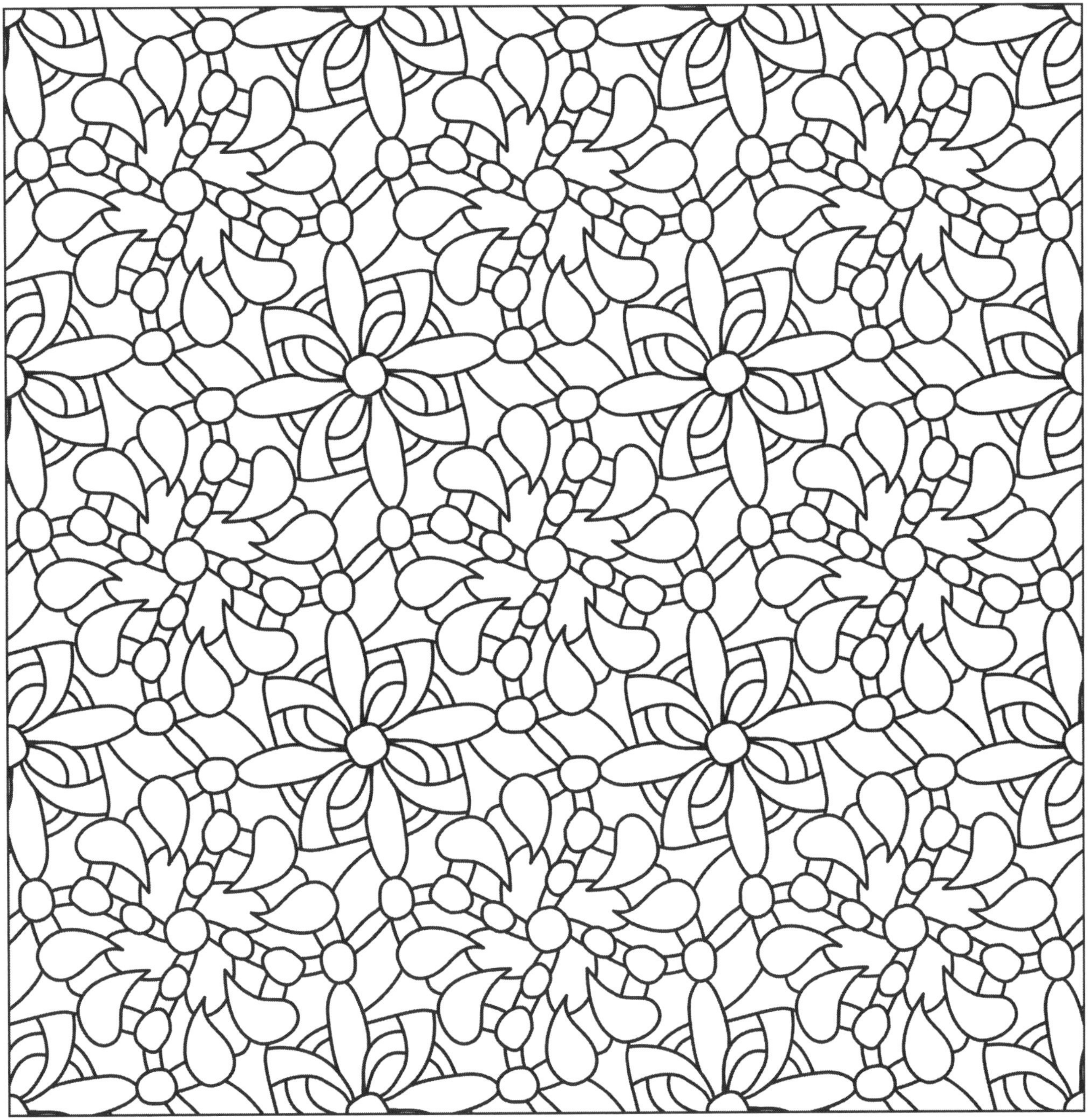

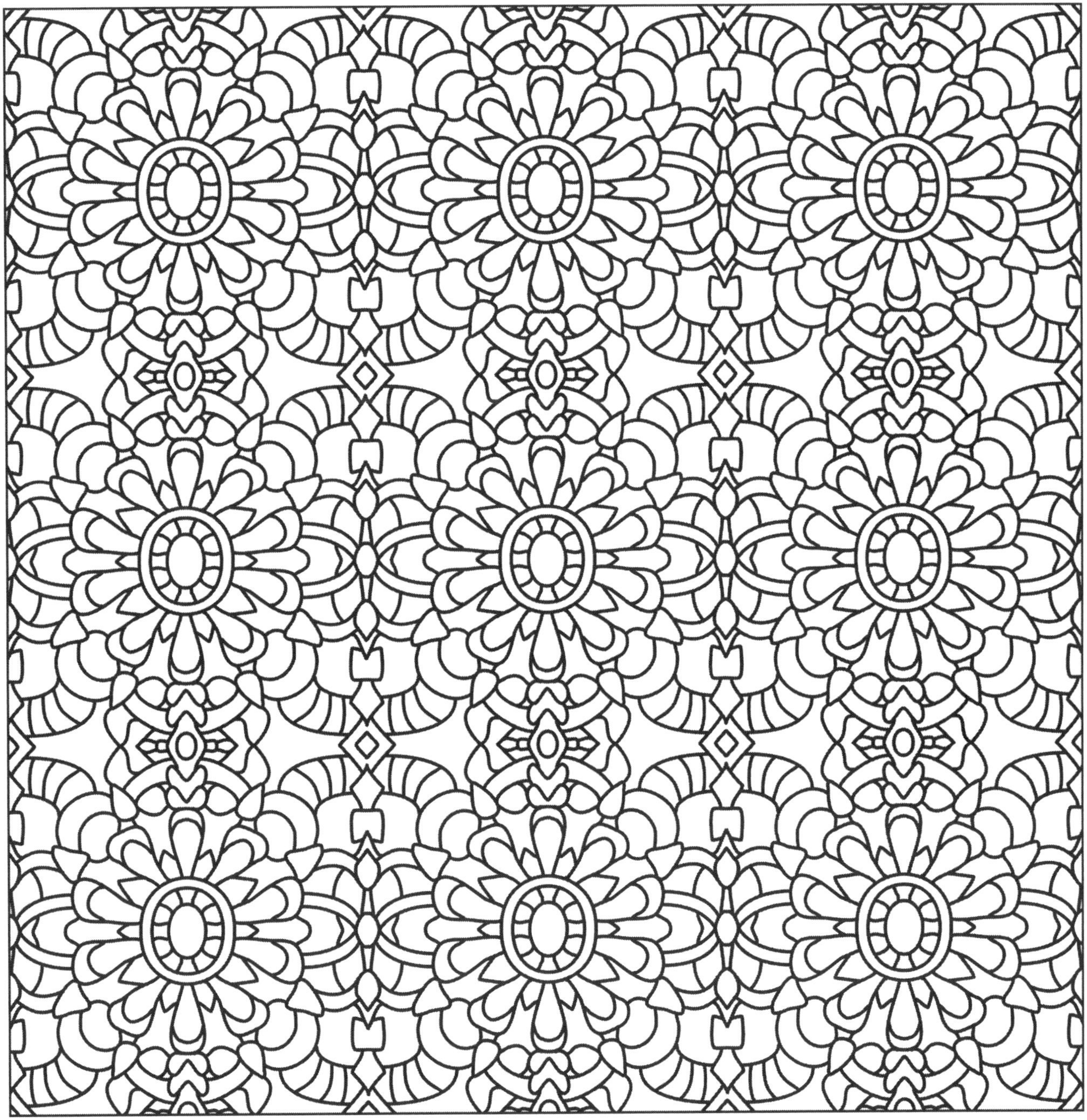

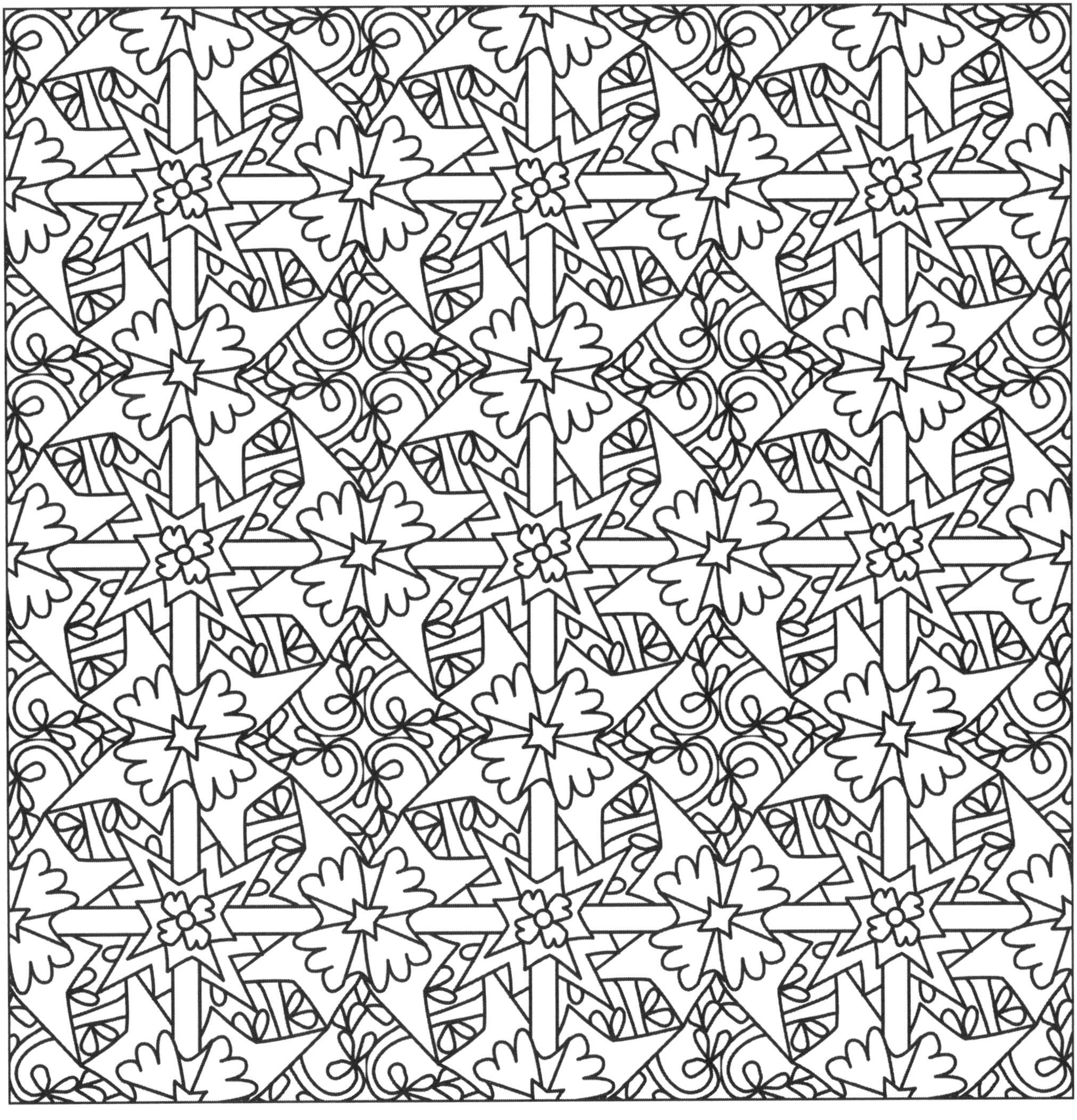

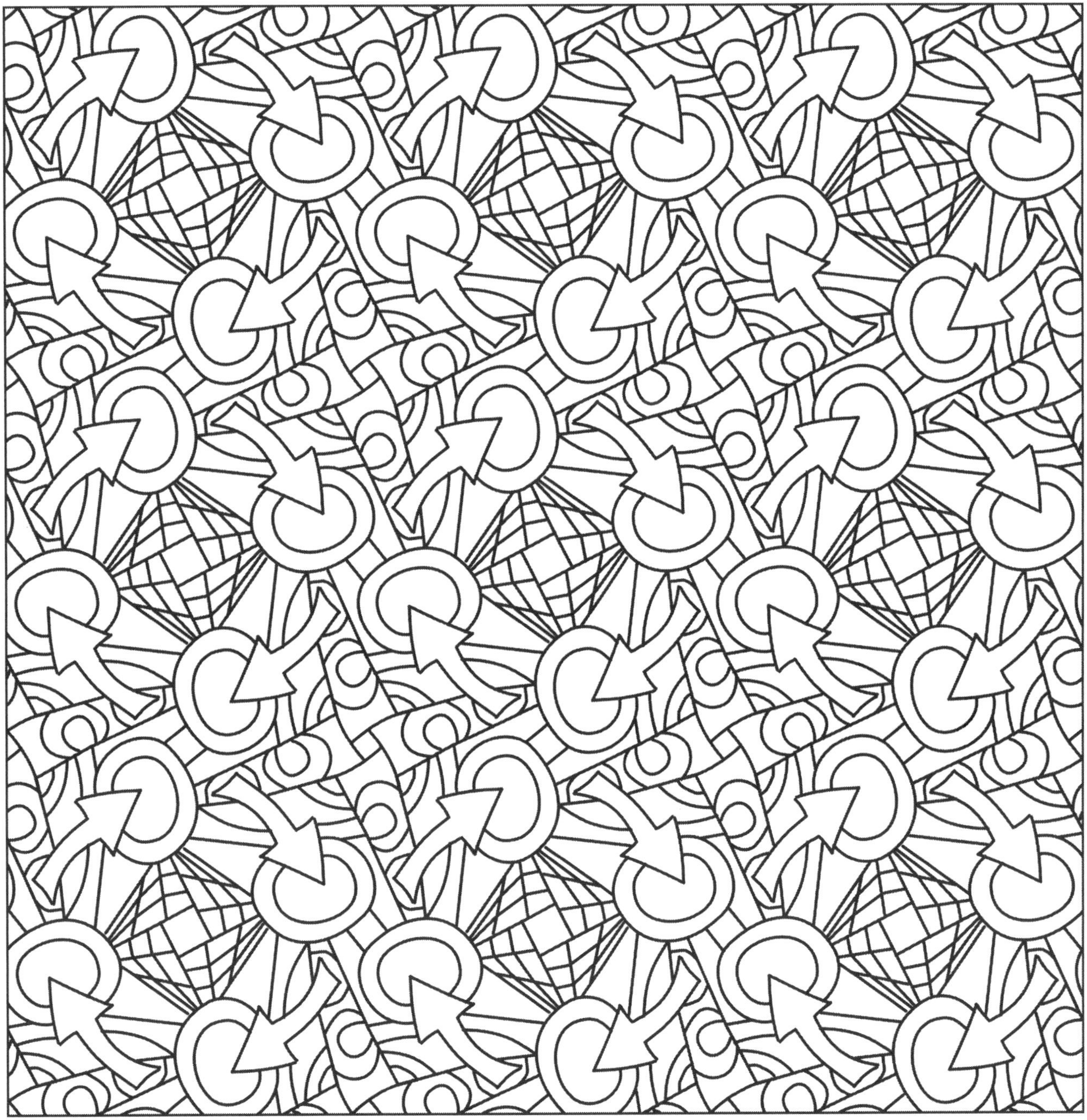

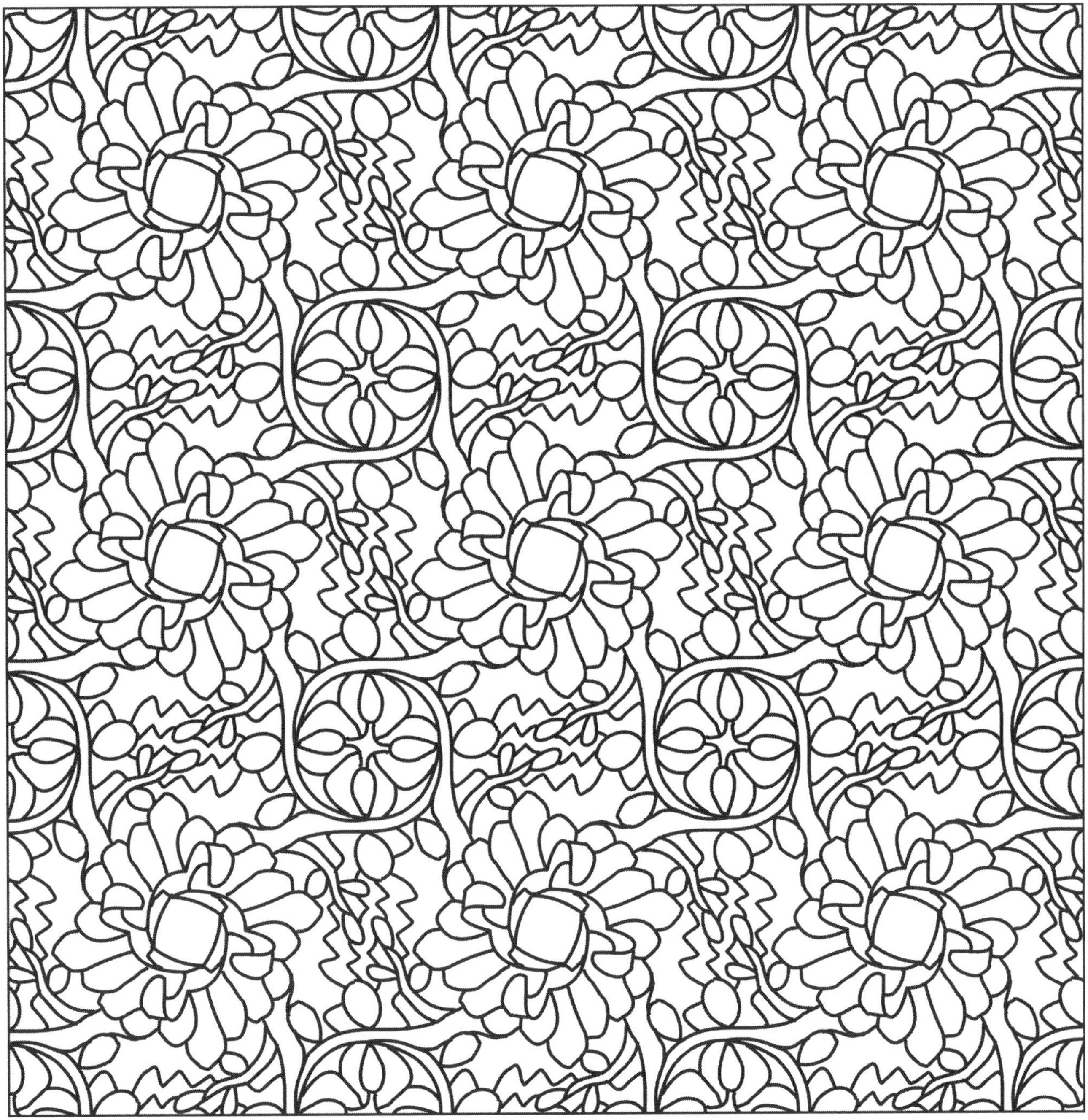

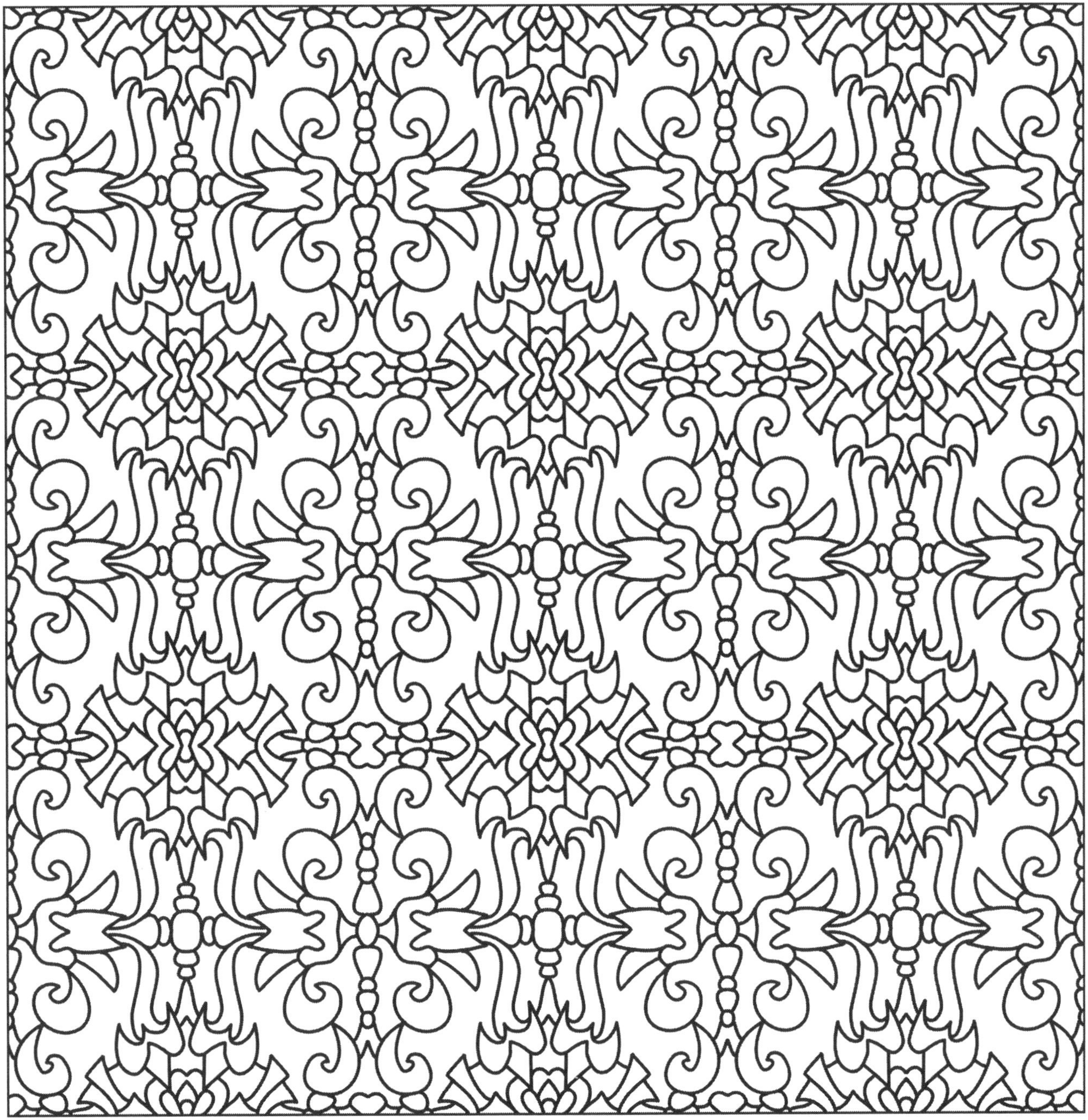

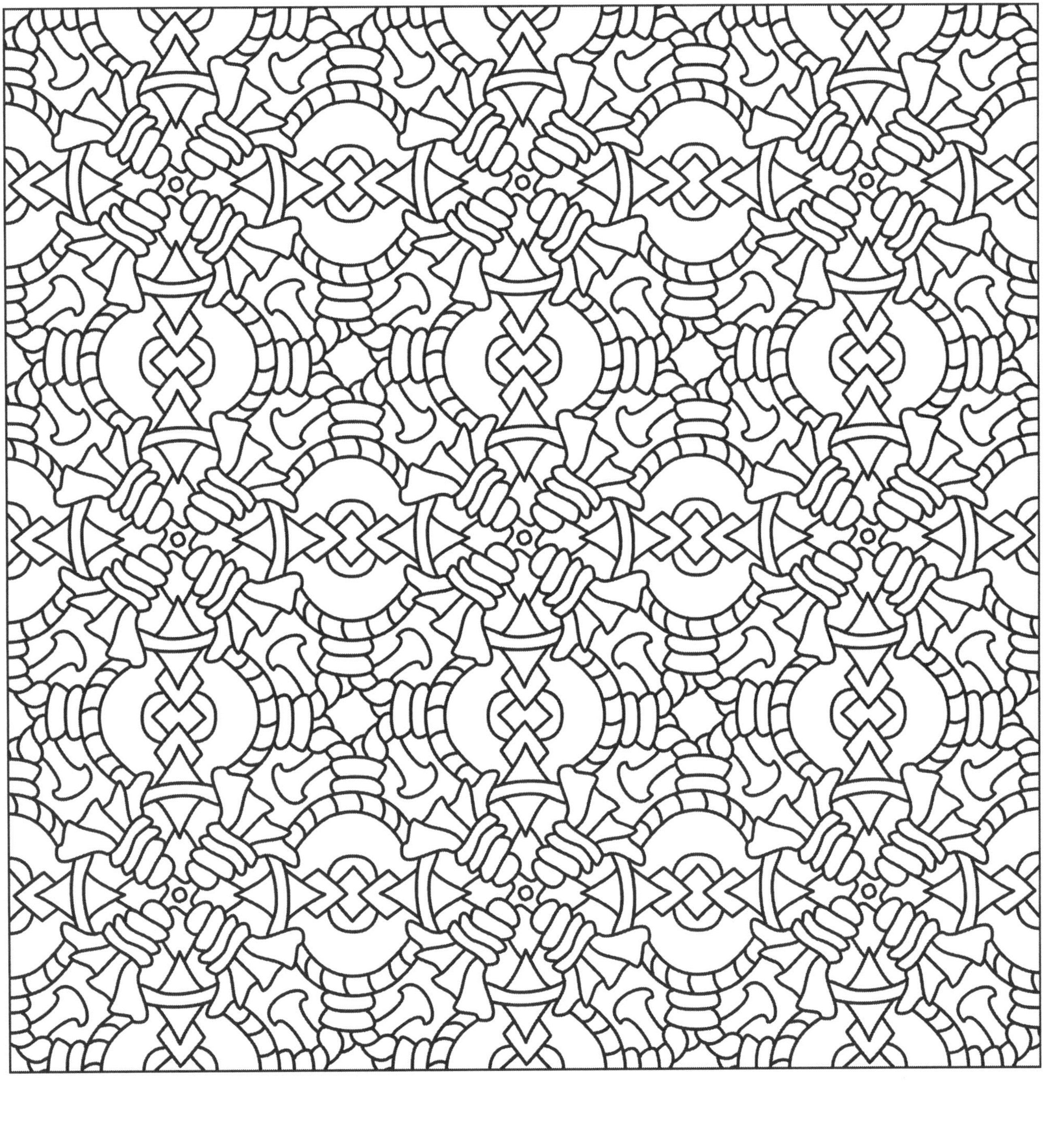

www.AngieGrace.com

Visit Angie's website for special web exclusives.